Legal Notices

Copyright Notice

Disclaimer

The content in **Illuminating the Path Within** is intended for informational and educational purposes only. The author and publisher are not licensed therapists, counselors, or medical professionals. The advice, exercises, and concepts presented in this book are based on personal experience and research. Readers are encouraged to seek professional advice or assistance if they have concerns regarding their mental, emotional, or physical health.

By engaging in the exercises or advice within this book, readers agree that they are solely responsible for their own well-being. The author and publisher shall not be held liable for any outcomes, adverse effects, or consequences resulting from the use or application of the information contained herein.

Legal Notice

This book is sold with the understanding that the author and publisher are not providing psychological, medical, legal, or any other professional advice. The information in this book does not constitute a substitute for professional services.

The Biblical Tarot Deck, as referenced in this book, is a tool for personal reflection and growth. It is not intended to predict future events or provide any guarantees. Readers are encouraged to use the deck responsibly and within the context of their own spiritual or personal journey.

Additional Notices

Trademark Notice: Any trademarks, service marks, product names, or named references within this book are the property of their respective owners. Their inclusion does not imply affiliation, sponsorship, or endorsement by these entities.

Third-Party Practices: The book may mention third-party tools, methods, or resources. These references are for informational purposes only. The author and publisher do not endorse or assume responsibility for these third-party materials.

Age Restriction: This book is intended for adult readers. Minors should only use this material under the supervision of a parent, guardian, or professional.

Religious Disclaimer: This book integrates Biblical themes and spiritual principles to aid shadow work and self-reflection. It is not intended to serve as a replacement for religious guidance or interpretations. Readers are encouraged to explore their spiritual beliefs independently and consult their faith leaders where appropriate.

Krasimir Kalin

illuminating
the
path
within

SHADOW WORK

with the Biblical Tarot

Shadows of the Soul

Table of Contents

Prologue

Unveiling the Shadows of the Soul

In the quiet moments of reflection, we sometimes encounter parts of ourselves we'd rather leave hidden—pieces of our soul we've denied, emotions we've buried, mistakes we've ignored. These hidden aspects form what psychologists call the "shadow." Though the term comes from modern psychology, the idea of confronting and transforming our inner darkness is ancient. In fact, it's woven into the fabric of the Bible itself.

This book is about shadow work, the deeply personal and spiritual journey of acknowledging, embracing, and transforming these hidden aspects of ourselves. Yet, it's more than just a psychological exercise; it's a sacred process rooted in ancient wisdom. Through the lens of biblical narratives, we'll explore how these time-honored stories mirror our inner struggles and can serve as a guiding light in the process of self-discovery.

The Bible offers more than a moral compass—it offers the blueprint for transformation. Figures like David, Moses, and Jacob wrestled with their flaws, their doubts, and their shadows. Through their stories, we find not only moral lessons but also a roadmap for confronting our own inner conflicts. This book will break down the process of shadow work into easy-to-follow steps, drawing on biblical wisdom to show how the moral values and teachings of Scripture can aid us in this journey.

The shadows in our lives are not to be feared; they are parts of us waiting to be understood, healed, and integrated. As you read through these pages, you will find that the path of shadow work is not a solitary struggle but one illuminated by faith, grace, and the timeless stories of those who came before us. It's a journey into the soul's depth—a journey toward wholeness, peace, and a deeper connection with the Divine.

This is not just a book about self-improvement; it's a guide to spiritual awakening through the wisdom of the Bible. It invites you to look beyond the surface of your being, to uncover the shadows, and to find the light within. Together, we will walk the path of transformation, guided by Scripture, and supported by the lessons from biblical figures who, like us, sought redemption, healing, and the courage to face their innermost selves.

Welcome to the Shadows of the Soul.

Part I

From Darkness to Light:

Unveiling and Overcoming the Shadows

Chapter 1

The Purpose of This Book

– A Journey
Beyond Negativity

What is the key to lasting transformation—positive thinking or the removal of negativity? This is a question many have pondered, but let us pause and ask: which holds greater power over your life? Is it the positive affirmations you repeat to yourself, or the silent, often unnoticed stream of negative thoughts that run in the background?

Research and human experience suggest that removing negative thinking is far more impactful than forcing positivity. This is because true positivity cannot flourish when negativity dominates our subconscious mind. Yet, negative thinking is so deeply embedded in our lives that we are often unaware of its presence. This book is not about slapping a layer of positivity over unresolved pain—it is about addressing negativity at its roots, uncovering hidden patterns, and transforming your inner world from the ground up.

The Illusion of Positive Thinking

Society often promotes the idea that thinking positively is the key to happiness and success. "Just stay positive," we are told. While this advice is well-meaning, it can feel hollow and even frustrating when deeper struggles remain unresolved. Positive thinking, on its own, can only go so far if it's not supported by a genuine sense of peace and self-acceptance.

Positive thinking is only effective when it's genuine and not an attempt to cover up unresolved pain or negativity. If negative thinking remains unaddressed, forced positivity can feel hollow and inauthentic.

Imagine someone who struggles with self-doubt. They might try to affirm, "I am confident and capable," but if they harbor a deep, unresolved fear of failure, the affirmation feels false. Their mind rejects it because the negative beliefs—rooted in fear, past criticism, or experiences—still dominate. It's only by addressing the root causes of their doubt that they can create space for genuine confidence and positivity to grow.

The Destructive Power of Negative Thinking

Negative thinking is so ingrained in our subconscious that we rarely notice how much it influences our lives. These thoughts often masquerade as truths, shaping how we see ourselves, others, and the world. Over time, they create patterns that can limit our potential, distort our relationships, and keep us trapped in cycles of self-doubt and fear.

Consider how often you find yourself thinking:

- "I'll never be good enough."
- "What if everything goes wrong?"
- "I always mess things up."

These thoughts may seem small, but they have profound effects. Left unchecked, they reinforce limiting beliefs, erode self-confidence, and prevent us from taking meaningful steps toward growth.

The Unconscious Nature of Negativity: Much of this negative thinking operates below the surface, in the subconscious mind. You may not even realize you're engaging in it until its effects become obvious—anxiety, procrastination, or even physical exhaustion. This is why bringing these patterns to light is essential.

Why Removing Negativity Comes First

The truth is, positivity cannot take root until negativity is addressed. Trying to build a foundation of positive thinking on top of negative beliefs is like planting a garden in rocky soil—the seeds may sprout, but they will struggle to grow.

By identifying and addressing negative thinking, we create space for authentic positivity to flourish. This process requires:

- **Awareness:** Recognizing the patterns of negative thinking that hold you back.

- **Compassion:** Approaching yourself with kindness as you confront these patterns.

- **Courage:** Delving into the root causes of negativity, often buried in the subconscious, and understanding their origins.

Shadow work, as explored in this book, is the path to achieving this transformation. By working through hidden fears, limiting beliefs, and unresolved pain, you pave the way for a new mindset—one that isn't forced but flows naturally from a place of self-awareness and inner peace.

How to Overcome Negativity

This book is a guide for self-reflection, healing, and transformation. It is designed to help you:

Identify Negative Thought Patterns:

- Through shadow work, uncover the negative beliefs and fears that shape your thoughts and behaviors.

- Recognize how these patterns are connected to your subconscious and learn to bring them into awareness.

Understand the Root Causes of Negativity:

- Explore the origins of negative thinking—whether from past experiences, cultural conditioning, or inherited beliefs—and learn to challenge their validity.

- Use practical exercises, like journaling and tarot spreads, to deepen your understanding.

Transform Negativity into Growth:

- Shadow work teaches you to confront negativity with compassion, not judgment. By doing so, you can integrate suppressed emotions, rewrite limiting narratives, and move forward with clarity and confidence.

Create Space for Authentic Positivity:

- As you release negativity, you naturally make room for joy, self-acceptance, and empowerment. This book guides you to cultivate these qualities in a way that feels authentic and sustainable.

Use the Biblical Tarot as a Reflective Tool:

- Each card in the Biblical Tarot embodies archetypes and lessons that reflect the human experience. By working with these cards, you'll gain insights into your shadows and learn how to transform them into strengths.

A New Approach to Inner Transformation

This book challenges the idea that positivity alone is the answer to life's struggles. Instead, it invites you to embark on a deeper journey— one that begins with acknowledging and transforming the negativity that has quietly shaped your life. This process is not about rejecting positivity; it's about creating the conditions for positivity to arise naturally, from a place of authenticity and balance.

By the end of this journey, you'll find that true transformation is not about forcing yourself to think positively but about freeing yourself from the weight of negativity. In doing so, you'll uncover the genuine peace, confidence, and joy that were always within you, waiting to emerge.

Chapter 2

Breaking the Chains

– Plato's Allegory of the Cave and Shadow Work

Imagine a dark cave where prisoners are chained, their bodies fixed so they can only face a blank wall. They have been there all their lives, knowing no other reality. Behind them burns a fire, and between the fire and the prisoners, people walk, carrying objects that cast shadows on the wall in front of them. To the prisoners, these shadows are the entire world. They cannot see the fire, the people, or the objects—only the flickering shapes projected on the wall. The shadows are their truth, a distorted version of reality they never question.

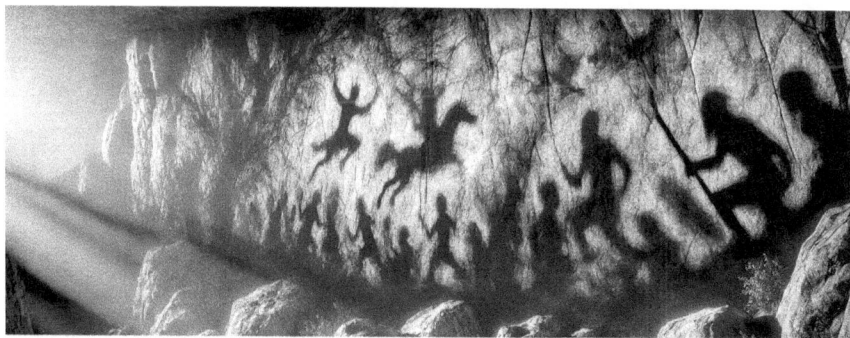

This is Plato's Allegory of the Cave, a profound metaphor for the human experience found in ***"The Republic"***. Through it, Plato illustrates the journey from ignorance to enlightenment. For those engaged in shadow work, this story resonates deeply, mirroring the process of confronting illusions, breaking free from the comfort of the familiar, and embracing the light of truth and self-awareness.

In the allegory, one prisoner breaks free. As he turns around, he sees the fire for the first time, realizing the shadows are not reality but mere reflections of something greater. The journey doesn't stop there—he ascends out of the cave into the light of the sun. At first, the brightness blinds him, but as his eyes adjust, he begins to see the world as it truly is, filled with color, depth, and vivid reality. Transformed by this experience, he feels compelled to return to the cave to share his discovery. Yet the other prisoners resist him, clinging to their familiar shadows, unwilling to confront the discomfort of the unknown.

Plato's allegory reflects a universal truth: we all live in some version of the cave, bound by chains of illusion and shaped by shadows. In the context of shadow work, the cave represents the mind's hidden corners, where suppressed fears, unresolved emotions, and limiting beliefs reside. The shadows on the wall are the distorted truths we accept—stories like "I'm not good enough," "I have no choice," or "This is who I must be." The fire behind us symbolizes the light of awareness, while the journey out of the cave mirrors the process of self-discovery and integration.

For many, the chains are built from fear. Like the prisoners, we may resist turning away from the shadows because they are familiar, even if they keep us stuck. The shadows represent the aspects of ourselves we project onto others or suppress in denial, believing it's safer not to look too closely. But shadow work begins with courage—the willingness to turn toward the fire and examine what lies beyond the comforting illusions.

Breaking free from these chains is the first step. Recognizing that the shadows we perceive are not the full truth is the beginning of the journey. This realization, however, is often uncomfortable. Just as the freed prisoner's eyes are overwhelmed by the sunlight, confronting our shadow self can be disorienting and painful. But this discomfort is necessary for growth. It signals that we are shedding illusions and moving closer to clarity and wholeness.

The journey out of the cave mirrors the transformative power of shadow work. As we confront our fears and integrate the aspects of ourselves we have denied, we ascend toward greater self-awareness. Each step requires courage and resilience, but it also brings profound rewards—freedom, authenticity, and the ability to perceive life in its fullness. Through shadow work, we gain the strength to face challenges with clarity and embrace the truth of who we are.

Remaining in the cave might feel safe, but it limits our potential for spiritual growth and personal fulfillment. Staying bound to the shadows perpetuates inner conflict and emotional stagnation. Breaking free is not about abandoning comfort but about finding a deeper, more meaningful existence beyond it. By confronting the shadows, we learn to see ourselves clearly, transforming old patterns and embracing the light of new possibilities.

The Biblical Tarot: Shadows of the Soul serves as a powerful tool for navigating this journey. Its archetypal imagery reflects both the shadows we carry and the light we seek. Cards like The Shadow (Jacob Wrestling with God) capture the struggle of facing inner truths, while The Tower embodies the destruction of illusions that no longer serve us. The Star, with its gentle light, offers hope and guidance, reminding us of the divine presence that illuminates even the darkest paths. Through the deck, we are invited to confront our shadows and ascend toward spiritual clarity and growth.

Plato's allegory teaches us that freedom lies not in clinging to illusions but in breaking the chains that bind us. The journey out of the cave requires effort, courage, and the willingness to face discomfort, but the rewards are immense. It is through this process that we move closer to the light, transforming not only our inner worlds but also the lives we touch. Shadow work is the modern embodiment of this timeless wisdom, offering a path from ignorance to enlightenment, from darkness to light. By embracing it, we take our first steps out of the cave and into the fullness of our potential.

Chapter 3

The Subconscious:

Unseen Currents That Shape Our Lives

Beneath the surface of our conscious awareness lies a vast and mysterious force—the subconscious mind. Like an ocean beneath a calm sky, it moves unseen, shaping the terrain of our lives in ways we seldom realize. It is this quiet operator that regulates our heartbeat, keeps our lungs breathing, balances our temperature, and ensures that we exist without effort or thought. Yet, its power does not stop with our physical being; it extends to every decision we make, every habit we hold, and every reaction we give.

The subconscious is both a faithful servant and an unyielding master, guiding us along paths laid out long before we are aware. Just as riding a bicycle or driving a car becomes second nature through practice, the subconscious internalizes our actions, turning them into automatic patterns. This is why you can hold a conversation while steering a vehicle or walk a familiar route without thinking about every step. But this same efficiency can also ensnare us in less beneficial loops—negative habits and beliefs formed in the past that linger in the shadows, influencing us without our consent.

Consider the subconscious as a vast archive of every experience you've ever had. It remembers not only your triumphs but also your fears, failures, and wounds. Over time, these experiences layer upon one another, forming habits, reactions, and beliefs that whisper to you in moments of decision. When left unexamined, these whispers become commands, shaping your choices and your life itself. The subconscious, then, is like a shadowy puppet master, guiding your actions without revealing its strings.

And what of free will? Are we truly free if so much of our behavior is dictated by subconscious patterns? The truth is, until we bring the contents of our subconscious into the light, we live as captives to its silent rule. Past traumas, societal expectations, and long-forgotten lessons from childhood all linger within, creating a maze of invisible barriers. A person who was once told they weren't good enough might hesitate to pursue opportunities, all the while unaware of the buried belief holding them back. This is not freedom; it is a life lived in the chains of unexamined thought.

Negative habits and beliefs, deeply rooted in the subconscious, don't remain hidden forever. Like messages in a bottle tossed into the ocean, they eventually wash ashore, sometimes in subtle ways. Perhaps you feel an unexplainable tension in certain situations, or you react with fear or anger before understanding why. Dreams, emotions, and recurring life patterns are often the subconscious trying to speak, revealing the hidden forces that shape your reality.

But the subconscious is not an enemy to be defeated—it is a companion to be understood. Communication with it must be a dialogue, a two-way street. If left to its own devices, it will dictate your life through old programming. But when engaged with intention and love, it becomes a powerful ally in rewriting your story. Tools like meditation, journaling, or the Biblical Tarot can serve as bridges to this hidden world, allowing you to decode its language and reshape its influence.

Imagine your subconscious as a garden. Left untended, weeds—negative habits, fears, and beliefs—thrive, overshadowing the flowers of potential. But with care, the soil can be tilled, the weeds removed, and the garden restored to a place of beauty and abundance. This is the work of reclaiming your free will—not by fighting the subconscious but by working with it to create a life aligned with your highest self.

The power of the subconscious is vast, but its grip on your life need not be absolute. By recognizing its influence, you can begin the process of liberation. With patience and intention, you can uncover the shadows that hold you back, break free from their chains, and step into a life of conscious choice. The subconscious is not your master; it is the silent force waiting to become your greatest ally. The question is, will you listen?

Chapter 4

Further into the Subconscious:

Veiled Depths of the Soul

Beneath the surface of our everyday awareness lies the subconscious mind, a vast reservoir of thoughts, memories, and emotions that influence how we think, feel, and behave. While the conscious mind deals with our immediate thoughts and decisions, the subconscious is responsible for storing everything we've experienced but may not be fully aware of. It is here, in the depths of the subconscious, where much of our shadow resides.

The subconscious mind is like an underground stream, constantly flowing beneath the surface. It holds onto the beliefs we've developed over time, often without us realizing it. Many of these beliefs come from early childhood, past experiences, societal conditioning, and traumas. As a result, the subconscious houses both the positive and negative aspects of our personality, including the parts of ourselves we suppress, ignore, or deny—the shadow.

In many ways, our shadows are the hidden aspects of our subconscious that influence us in profound ways. Unresolved emotions, repressed memories, and unexamined fears may bubble up into our conscious awareness in the form of anxiety, self-sabotage, or relationship conflicts. This is why shadow work and the exploration of the subconscious are deeply interconnected—by understanding the subconscious, we begin to understand our shadows.

When the Subconscious Becomes a Silent Obstacle

Our subconscious can hinder our lives in ways we don't always recognize. Because it holds onto unexamined parts of ourselves, it influences our decisions, behaviors, and reactions without us being fully aware of it. When our shadow is unaddressed, it often shows up in the following ways:

- **Repeating Patterns of Self-Sabotage:**
  One of the most common ways our subconscious hinders us is through patterns of self-sabotage. This happens when subconscious beliefs about ourselves—often rooted in fear, shame, or unworthiness—lead us to make choices that undermine our goals and well-being. For example, someone who subconsciously believes they are unworthy of love may push away relationships, even though they consciously desire connection.

- **Emotional Triggers:**
  Our shadows often manifest in emotional triggers—moments when we have an outsized reaction to a situation. These triggers are the subconscious surfacing unresolved emotions or traumas. For example, if someone is overly defensive in conversations, it may stem from a subconscious fear of being judged or rejected.

- **Limiting Beliefs:**
  Subconscious shadows are also responsible for limiting beliefs—ideas we hold about ourselves that restrict our potential. These beliefs, such as "I'm not good enough"

or "I can't succeed," often stem from early life experiences or societal conditioning. When these beliefs remain unchecked, they limit our ability to grow, thrive, and achieve our goals.

- **Unfulfilled Potential:**
  Perhaps the most significant consequence of an unexamined shadow is that it prevents us from realizing our full potential. The energy we spend suppressing parts of ourselves could instead be used to live authentically and pursue our purpose. As long as the subconscious shadows remain hidden, they act as barriers to personal and spiritual growth.

The Role of the Biblical Tarot in Connecting with the Subconscious

The Biblical Tarot: Shadows of the Soul is a powerful tool designed to help you access the subconscious mind and uncover the hidden aspects of yourself—your shadows. Tarot, by its very nature, speaks the language of the subconscious. Each card is like a mirror, reflecting not just conscious thoughts but also the deeper, unseen layers of our inner world.

Here's how the Biblical Tarot: Shadows of the Soul can aid in the process of connecting with your subconscious and realizing your shadows:

Symbolism as a Gateway to the Subconscious:

The subconscious mind communicates through symbols, images, and stories, rather than direct thoughts or words. This is why the symbolic nature of tarot is so powerful. Each card in the Biblical Tarot: Shadows of the Soul contains a biblical story or character, offering rich symbolism that speaks directly to the subconscious. These symbols help bypass the logical, analytical mind and tap into the deeper layers of our psyche.

For example, when you draw a card like "Jacob Wrestles with God," your subconscious immediately connects the symbolism of this struggle to your own inner conflicts. You may not consciously realize what part of yourself you're wrestling with, but the card helps bring that subconscious struggle into awareness. The story of Jacob becomes a reflection of your own battle with your shadow.

Bringing the Subconscious into Conscious Awareness:

Tarot spreads are structured in such a way that they allow you to bring your subconscious thoughts, emotions, and beliefs into conscious awareness. When you ask a question or focus on a specific aspect of your shadow work while drawing cards, the cards you pull often reveal hidden truths about your subconscious.

For instance, if you ask, "What shadow is blocking my spiritual growth?" and draw the card of "Peter's Denial of Christ," the message may point to feelings of shame or fear of rejection that you've buried in your subconscious. This is something you may not have consciously recognized, but the card allows you to see it clearly.

The process of shadow work requires this level of awareness—identifying what's hidden so that it can be addressed and healed. The Biblical Tarot: Shadows of the Soul acts as a bridge between the conscious and subconscious, illuminating the parts of yourself that you've kept in the dark.

Identifying the Chains That Bind Your Life

Through regular use of the Biblical Tarot: Shadows of the Soul, you can start to identify the specific shadows that are hindering your life. The cards help you explore the recurring themes, patterns, and beliefs that are preventing you from fully embracing your potential. Each biblical story offers a lesson or reflection that sheds light on the subconscious influences shaping your life.

For example, drawing the "Moses and the Burning Bush" card in reverse could reveal that you're avoiding a calling or opportunity due to fear or self-doubt. By connecting with this story on a subconscious level, you start to realize that your fear of stepping into the unknown is the shadow that's been holding you back.

The more you engage with the deck, the clearer these shadows become. The cards don't just show you what's hindering your life; they also offer spiritual guidance on how to overcome these obstacles. Biblical figures who faced their own trials, temptations, and flaws provide a blueprint for addressing the shadows in your subconscious.

Realizing Our Shadows: The Path to Healing and Growth

By connecting with your subconscious through the Biblical Tarot: Shadows of the Soul, you gain the awareness needed to bring your shadows into the light. Awareness is the first step toward transformation. Once you realize what has been hindering your life—whether it's fear, shame, guilt, or limiting beliefs—you can begin the process of healing and growth.

Each card in the deck acts as a guide on this journey, pointing out the hidden influences that have been shaping your decisions, behaviors, and relationships. As you continue to work with the deck, you become more adept at recognizing these subconscious patterns and shadows, allowing you to make conscious choices that align with your true self.

The Bible's teachings on self-examination, repentance, and redemption are echoed in the practice of shadow work. As you realize and confront your shadows, you are not just engaging in psychological healing—you are also engaging in a spiritual practice of transformation. By bringing the subconscious into the light of awareness, you align yourself more fully with God's purpose for your life.

Conclusion: Awakening the Subconscious to Heal the Shadow

The subconscious mind holds many of the keys to understanding the shadow. It is where our deepest fears, beliefs, and unresolved emotions reside. By connecting with the subconscious through the Biblical Tarot: Shadows of the Soul, we are able to unlock the hidden parts of ourselves that have been hindering our lives and spiritual growth.

The journey of shadow work is one of awakening—of bringing the hidden into the light, of realizing our shadows, and of transforming them into sources of strength and wisdom. With the help of the tarot, we learn to see ourselves more clearly, embrace our flaws, and live in greater alignment with both our true selves and the teachings of the Bible.

Chapter 5

The Journey of the Soul

– A Path of Discovery, Healing, and Growth

What is the Journey of the Soul?

The journey of the soul is the sacred path each of us undertakes from the moment we are born. It is the journey through life, where we encounter choices, challenges, opportunities, and growth. In the Biblical Tarot: Shadows of the Soul, this journey is represented by The Soul card, which replaces the traditional Fool card. The Soul card marks the beginning of our personal and spiritual development, symbolizing the infinite potential within us and the unique challenges we will face along the way.

The journey of the soul is not a straight line. It is a path of discovery—one filled with lessons, trials, and transformations. Along this path, we face both light and shadow, joy and suffering, all of which shape us into who we are meant to be. Every experience, every choice, every relationship becomes a stepping stone toward self-awareness and spiritual growth.

In this journey, we are called to explore the depths of our inner selves, confront the shadows we've hidden away, and bring them into the light. It is a process of becoming whole—of integrating all parts of ourselves, both light and dark, so that we can live in alignment with our highest purpose.

Why It Is Important to Embark on This Journey of Self-Discovery and Development

Embarking on the journey of the soul is essential for personal growth and spiritual fulfillment. Self-discovery allows us to move beyond the surface of our everyday lives and explore the deeper motivations, fears, and desires that shape our actions. Without this inner exploration, we risk living unconsciously—reacting to life's challenges based on patterns we don't fully understand. But when we engage with this journey, we gain clarity, insight, and the ability to make choices that are aligned with our true selves.

Here's why this journey is so important:

1. Self-Awareness Leads to Personal Freedom

By understanding our inner world—our thoughts, emotions, and patterns—we free ourselves from being controlled by unconscious forces. We gain the ability to choose how we respond to life, rather than being driven by fear, insecurity, or unresolved wounds. Self-awareness brings us closer to personal freedom, as we become more conscious of the choices we make and the power we hold in shaping our lives.

2. Growth Through Adversity

The journey of the soul is not without its challenges. But it is through facing these challenges that we grow. Just as a tree's roots grow deeper during a storm, we too grow stronger by confronting the difficulties in our lives. The shadows we face—our fears, doubts, and insecurities—are opportunities for growth and transformation. By embracing them, we develop resilience, wisdom, and compassion.

3. Living Authentically

When we embark on the journey of self-discovery, we begin to strip away the layers of conditioning, expectations, and limiting beliefs that have held us back. We get closer to our true selves—our authentic nature. This allows us to live in greater alignment with our values, passions, and purpose. Living authentically brings a sense of fulfillment, peace, and joy that can only come from being true to who we are.

4. Connection to the Divine

The journey of the soul is also a spiritual journey. It is through this process that we come closer to understanding our relationship with the Divine. As we grow in self-awareness and heal our shadows, we create space for a deeper connection with God. This journey is about aligning our lives with a higher purpose, walking in faith, and trusting that we are being guided every step of the way.

The Journey from the Perspective of Psychology, the Bible, and Tarot

The Biblical Tarot: Shadows of the Soul deck beautifully integrates three powerful frameworks for understanding the journey of the soul—Psychology, the Bible, and Tarot. Each perspective offers unique insights into our path of growth and transformation, and when combined, they create a holistic approach to self-discovery and healing.

1. The Journey of the Soul through Psychology

From the perspective of psychology, the journey of the soul involves exploring the conscious and unconscious mind. Carl Jung, the psychologist most associated with the concept of shadow work, believed that we must confront and integrate our shadows—the hidden parts of ourselves that we repress or deny—in order to become whole. Psychology teaches us that much of our behavior is driven by unconscious patterns formed early in life. These patterns can keep us stuck in cycles of fear, self-sabotage, and emotional reactivity.

By applying psychological principles to the journey of the soul, we begin to uncover the unconscious beliefs and emotions that shape our lives. This involves doing the inner work—reflecting on our past, identifying our triggers, and healing the wounds that have influenced our behavior. Psychology helps us understand that the soul's journey is not just a spiritual one but also a deeply psychological one. The more we understand our inner world, the more we can navigate life's challenges with clarity and purpose.

The Biblical Tarot incorporates this psychological approach by encouraging reflection and self-examination through each card. When we draw cards like the Shadow or The Soul, we are prompted to explore our hidden fears, unresolved emotions, and personal growth opportunities. The deck invites us to take an active role in our psychological healing.

2. The Journey of the Soul through the Bible

The Bible offers profound insights into the journey of the soul, with stories of transformation, redemption, and spiritual growth woven throughout its pages. From the struggles of Jacob to the perseverance of Job, the Bible reminds us that the path to spiritual fulfillment is not without trials. But it also teaches that through faith, grace, and redemption, we can overcome the obstacles that stand in our way.

In the biblical context, the journey of the soul is about becoming more aligned with God's purpose for our lives. It involves repentance, forgiveness, and transformation. We are called to confront our weaknesses, not in shame, but with the trust that God's grace will guide us toward healing and wholeness. The Bible provides the moral and spiritual foundation for shadow work, reminding us that God sees all parts of us—our light and our shadows—and loves us fully.

The Biblical Tarot uses these biblical stories and teachings to guide us on our journey. When we draw cards representing biblical figures or stories, we are reminded of the spiritual lessons embedded in their lives. We see how their struggles mirror our own and how their faith led them through times of darkness. The Bible serves as a roadmap, offering us guidance as we walk our own path of self-discovery and spiritual growth.

3. The Journey of the Soul through Tarot

Tarot, at its core, is a symbolic representation of the journey through life. The traditional tarot deck tells the story of the Fool's journey—a journey of growth, learning, and transformation. In the Biblical Tarot, this journey is represented by The Soul card, which highlights the unique challenges and opportunities we encounter as spiritual beings on Earth.

Tarot invites us to engage with our inner wisdom and intuition. Each card offers a symbolic reflection of our inner world, helping us uncover hidden truths, face our shadows, and make empowered choices. The Biblical Tarot adds a spiritual dimension to this practice by aligning these symbols with biblical teachings, offering not only psychological insight but also spiritual guidance.

By using Tarot as a tool for reflection, we gain access to our subconscious mind—the part of ourselves that holds the key to our hidden fears, desires, and potential. The Biblical Tarot: Shadows of the Soul invites us to engage with these symbols in a way that blends intuition, spirituality, and personal growth, offering a comprehensive approach to self-discovery.

A Path to Wholeness

Combining the perspectives of psychology, the Bible, and tarot provides a powerful framework for the journey of the soul. Each of these elements contributes something essential to the process:

- Psychology gives us the tools to explore the unconscious mind, heal past wounds, and develop greater self-awareness.

- The Bible offers spiritual guidance, reminding us that we are never alone in our struggles and that God's grace is always available to us.

- Tarot serves as a symbolic mirror, helping us access our intuition and navigate the complexities of our inner world.

Together, these approaches create a balanced path toward wholeness. By integrating the wisdom of psychology, the moral and spiritual teachings of the Bible, and the intuitive insights of tarot, we are better equipped to face the challenges of the soul's journey. We gain a deeper understanding of ourselves, a stronger connection to the Divine, and the tools to heal and grow.

Conclusion:
Walking the Path with Wisdom and Faith

The journey of the soul is one of discovery, healing, and transformation. As we walk this path, we are called to engage with our shadows, face our fears, and embrace our potential for growth. By combining the wisdom of psychology, the Bible, and tarot, we create a holistic approach to this journey—one that honors both our spiritual and psychological needs.

The Biblical Tarot: Shadows of the Soul is a guide on this journey, offering insight, wisdom, and encouragement as we navigate life's challenges and opportunities. With each card, we are reminded that the journey of the soul is sacred, and that through faith, reflection, and inner work, we can overcome the obstacles on our path and step into our true potential.

Chapter 6

Jung's Iceberg Theory

– A Framework for Shadow Work

To fully understand the process of shadow work, we must explore the profound insights of Carl Gustav Jung, a pioneering figure in psychology. Jung's work on the unconscious mind and his metaphor of the iceberg provide a powerful framework for understanding how the visible and hidden aspects of our psyche interact. This chapter delves into Jung's iceberg theory, explaining its significance in understanding the subconscious, the shadow, and the deeper dimensions of the self.

Who Was Carl Jung?

Carl Jung (1875–1961) was a Swiss psychiatrist and psychoanalyst, widely regarded as one of the most influential thinkers in modern psychology. A student of Sigmund Freud, Jung eventually broke away from Freud's theories to develop his own school of thought, known as analytical psychology. Jung's work emphasized the importance of the unconscious mind in shaping human behavior and introduced concepts like the collective unconscious, archetypes, and shadow.

Jung believed that psychological health requires integrating the hidden aspects of the self—both personal and collective—into conscious awareness. His iceberg theory offers a metaphorical lens for understanding the layers of the psyche, providing crucial insights into how we can engage with shadow work.

Understanding Jung's Iceberg Theory

Jung's iceberg theory presents the mind as an iceberg floating in the ocean. While a small portion of the iceberg (the conscious mind) is visible above the waterline, the vast majority lies submerged, representing the unconscious and subconscious aspects of the psyche.

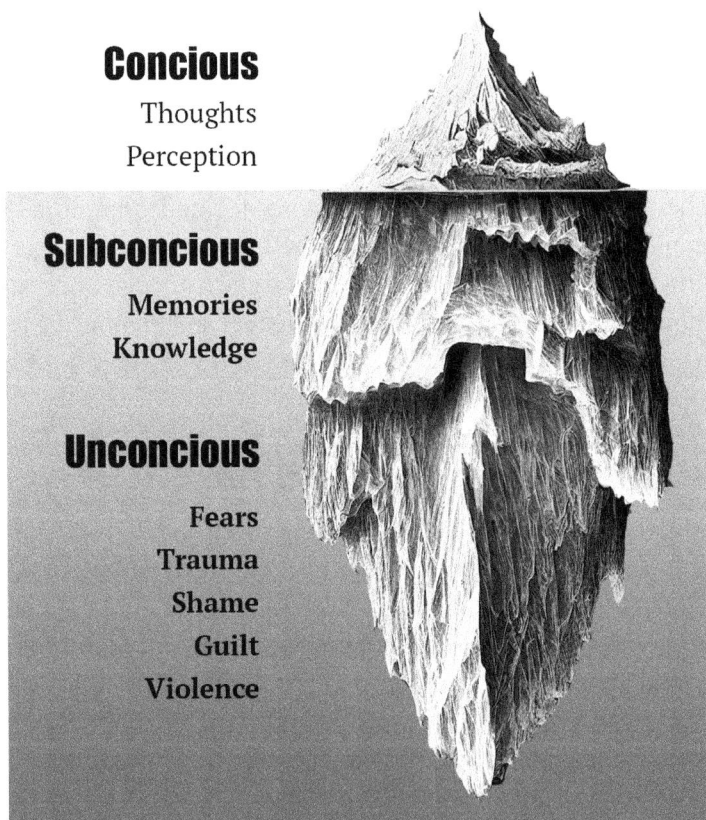

Concious
Thoughts
Perception

Subconcious
Memories
Knowledge

Unconcious
Fears
Trauma
Shame
Guilt
Violence

- **The Visible: The Conscious Mind**
  This is the part of the mind we are actively aware of—our thoughts, perceptions, decisions, and logical reasoning. It's where we focus our attention and engage with the external world. While important, the conscious mind represents only a fraction of the total psyche.

- **Just Below the Surface: The Subconscious Mind**
  The subconscious acts as a bridge between the conscious and unconscious. It stores information we aren't actively thinking about but can access when needed, such as memories, habits, and beliefs. It also houses many of our emotional reactions and conditioned responses, shaping our behavior without our explicit awareness.

- **The Vast Hidden Depths: The Unconscious Mind**
  The unconscious mind is the deepest layer of the iceberg, containing repressed memories, unresolved emotions, and the shadow. It is also home to Jung's archetypes—universal symbols and patterns that influence human behavior. The unconscious exerts a powerful influence on our lives, often driving thoughts and actions in ways we do not fully understand.

- **The Shadow Within the Iceberg**
  Jung described the shadow as the part of the unconscious mind that holds the traits, desires, and emotions we deny or suppress. These shadow aspects are often shaped by societal, cultural, or familial expectations that teach us which traits are acceptable and which must be hidden.

The shadow doesn't disappear when repressed; it lingers in the depths of the unconscious, influencing our behavior in subtle and often destructive ways. Left unexamined, it can create patterns of self-sabotage, recurring conflicts, or unexplainable fears.

Why the Iceberg Model Matters for Shadow Work

The iceberg model is essential for understanding shadow work because it illustrates how much of our inner world is hidden from conscious awareness. Shadow work is the process of bringing these hidden aspects to light, integrating them into the conscious mind to achieve greater self-awareness, wholeness, and freedom.

Key Insights from the Iceberg Model:

1. The Power of the Hidden:

The majority of our thoughts, feelings, and behaviors are influenced by the subconscious and unconscious mind. Understanding this helps us see that addressing surface-level issues is rarely enough for true transformation.

2. The Interconnectedness of the Psyche:

The conscious, subconscious, and unconscious minds are not separate entities but interconnected layers. Healing and growth require engaging with all layers of the psyche.

3. The Role of the Shadow:

The shadow resides in the depths of the unconscious, shaping our fears, desires, and behaviors. Bringing it into awareness is a transformative act, allowing us to reclaim hidden strengths and release unresolved pain.

4. The Need for Depth:

True self-awareness and healing require exploring the depths of the unconscious. By venturing below the surface, we uncover the beliefs, memories, and emotions that shape our lives.

Conclusion: Embracing the Depths

Jung's iceberg theory reminds us that the conscious mind is only the beginning of self-understanding. The true depths of the psyche—the subconscious and unconscious—hold the keys to transformation, healing, and wholeness. By acknowledging the hidden layers of our mind and engaging with the shadow, we gain access to the full spectrum of our humanity, embracing both the light and the dark.

As you journey through this book, remember the iceberg. Each layer you explore brings you closer to the authentic self that lies beneath the surface, waiting to be discovered.

Chapter 7

The Vibrational Frequency of Emotions

Emotions are not just fleeting feelings; they are powerful forces that influence every aspect of our lives. The concept of an Emotional Frequency Vibration Chart offers a framework to understand how our emotions impact our well-being, decisions, and interactions with the world. This chapter explores the origins of the emotional frequency chart, what it represents, and its importance in the process of shadow work and personal growth.

The Origins of the Emotional Frequency Chart

The idea of emotions as frequencies can be traced to the intersection of psychology, spirituality, and quantum physics. The concept gained popularity through the work of Dr. David R. Hawkins. He introduced the Map of Consciousness, which ranked emotional states on a vibrational scale based on their energy levels.

At its core, the chart reflects the idea that emotions are measurable vibrations, with low-frequency emotions like shame and fear corresponding to denser, more negative states, and high-frequency emotions like love and joy corresponding to expansive, uplifting states. While rooted in theoretical and experiential practices, the chart has become a widely used tool for self-awareness and healing.

What Is the Emotional Frequency Vibration Chart?

The Emotional Frequency Vibration Chart is a visual representation of emotional states, arranged from the lowest vibrations (associated with dense, negative emotions) to the highest (associated with light, positive emotions). It represents the energetic impact of emotions on the body, mind, and spirit.

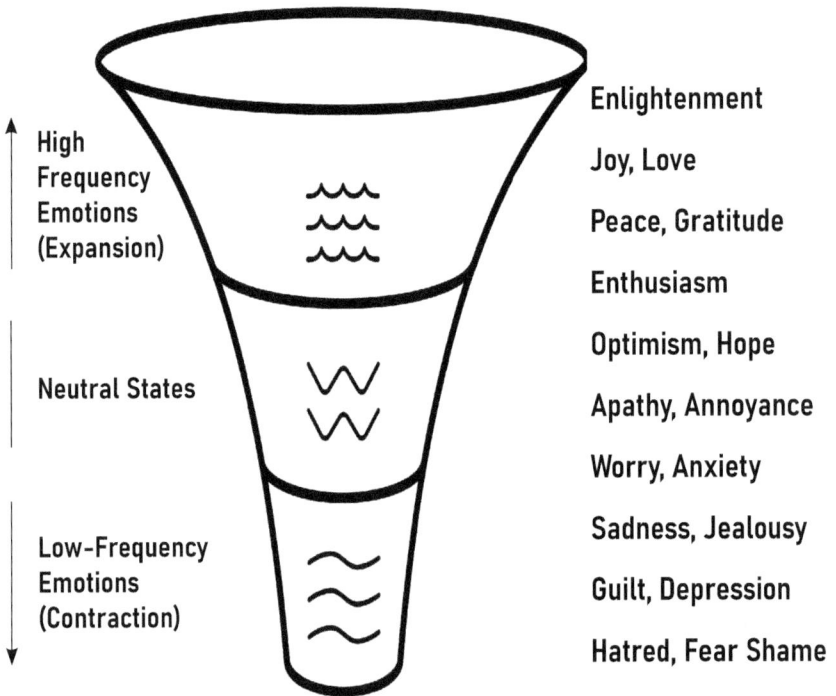

High Frequency Emotions (Expansion)

Neutral States

Low-Frequency Emotions (Contraction)

Enlightenment

Joy, Love

Peace, Gratitude

Enthusiasm

Optimism, Hope

Apathy, Annoyance

Worry, Anxiety

Sadness, Jealousy

Guilt, Depression

Hatred, Fear Shame

- **Low-Frequency Emotions:**
  Shame, guilt, apathy, and fear occupy the lower end of the scale. These emotions are constrictive, often linked to feelings of stagnation, helplessness, or disconnection.

- **Neutral States:**
  Emotions like acceptance and willingness mark the mid-point, where the energy begins to shift from constriction to expansion.

- **High-Frequency Emotions:**
  Love, joy, peace, and enlightenment occupy the top of the scale. These emotions are expansive, associated with growth, connection, and well-being.

The chart helps individuals recognize where they are emotionally and understand the vibrational impact of their feelings on their experiences.

Why Is Emotional State Important?

Our emotional state is the lens through which we experience life. It influences our thoughts, decisions, relationships, and physical health. Emotions serve as a feedback system, reflecting the alignment—or misalignment—between our conscious mind and deeper truths.

- **Emotions and Energy:** Emotions are energy in motion. High-frequency emotions elevate our energy, fostering clarity, creativity, and resilience. Low-frequency emotions drain our energy, creating blocks and resistance.

- **Emotions as Signals:** Negative emotions are not inherently bad; they serve as signals pointing to unresolved pain or unmet needs. By understanding these emotions, we can address their root causes rather than suppressing them.

- **Impact on Shadow Work:** Emotional states are deeply tied to the shadow. Low-frequency emotions often emerge from suppressed aspects of the self, such as shame, guilt, or fear. Recognizing and working through these emotions is a key part of shadow integration.

Emotional Spirals:
The Upward and Downward Cycle

Emotions are not static; they create spirals that can either lift us to greater heights or drag us into deeper negativity. Understanding these spirals is crucial for navigating emotional states and maintaining balance.

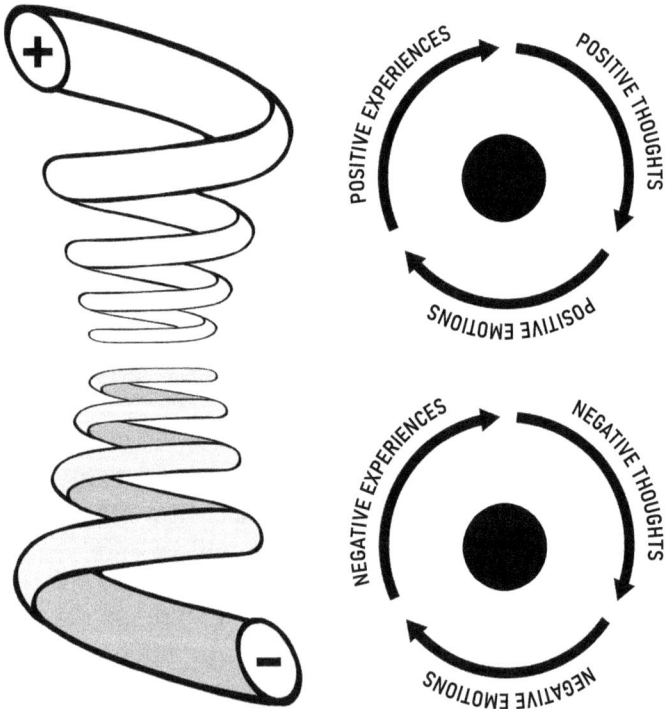

The Positive Spiral:

- Positive emotions, such as gratitude, joy, or hope, generate an upward spiral. Feeling good leads to more positive thoughts and behaviors, attracting uplifting experiences and relationships. This creates momentum for personal growth and well-being.

- **Example:** Starting the day with gratitude can set a positive tone, influencing how you perceive and respond to challenges.

The Negative Spiral:

- Negative emotions, like anger, fear, or despair, create a downward spiral. These emotions feed into negative thoughts and behaviors, perpetuating a cycle of disconnection, pain, and self-sabotage.

- **Example:** A small setback, like a mistake at work, can trigger self-critical thoughts, leading to feelings of inadequacy and further mistakes.

Why Balancing Emotional States Matters

Learning to balance your emotional state is essential for breaking free from negative spirals and maintaining a sense of well-being. This doesn't mean avoiding negative emotions but rather engaging with them consciously to prevent them from taking over.

- **Breaking the Negative Spiral:** Recognizing when you are in a downward spiral allows you to interrupt the pattern. Techniques like mindfulness, grounding, and self-compassion can help shift your energy and perspective.

- **Cultivating Emotional Resilience:** Balancing emotional states helps you respond to life's challenges with greater calm and clarity. Resilience comes from acknowledging all emotions—positive and negative—while choosing not to let negativity dominate.

- **Fostering Growth:** Emotional balance supports the shadow work process by creating a stable foundation for exploring and integrating hidden parts of the self. When balanced, you can face challenging emotions with curiosity and compassion.

The Emotional Frequency Chart in Shadow Work

The emotional frequency chart deepens our understanding of the mind by showing how emotions influence our thoughts, actions, and overall energy. In shadow work, it serves as a roadmap for recognizing and transforming low-frequency emotions that arise from suppressed parts of the self.

- **Recognizing Patterns:** Use the chart to identify recurring emotional states. Are you frequently experiencing guilt or fear? These emotions may point to unresolved aspects of your shadow.

- **Tracking Progress:** The chart can help you track your emotional growth. Moving from lower vibrations like anger to higher states like acceptance or joy reflects progress in shadow integration.

- **Encouraging Self-Awareness:** By understanding the vibrational impact of emotions, you become more attuned to how your feelings shape your experiences. This awareness empowers you to make conscious choices that align with your higher self.

Conclusion:
Emotions as the Key to Transformation

The Emotional Frequency Vibration Chart is more than a tool for self-awareness—it's a guide to understanding the energetic impact of emotions and their role in shaping our lives. By recognizing the spirals of positive and negative emotions, we gain insight into the patterns that influence our thoughts, behaviors, and relationships.

In the process of shadow work, the chart becomes a valuable companion. It helps us confront low-frequency emotions with compassion, transform them into sources of growth, and cultivate the high-frequency emotions that elevate our lives. By learning to balance our emotional state, we create a foundation for healing, self-discovery, and authentic joy.

Chapter 8

Exploring the Shadows

Shadow work is a transformative psychological and spiritual practice that involves confronting and integrating the parts of ourselves that we tend to repress or deny. These hidden parts—the "shadow"—often contain traits, emotions, or behaviors we don't want to acknowledge, such as anger, jealousy, fear, and guilt. However, the shadow isn't inherently negative. It simply holds the aspects of ourselves we haven't yet come to terms with. By bringing these hidden elements into conscious awareness, we allow ourselves the opportunity to heal, grow, and become more whole.

In many ways, shadow work is a process of self-acceptance. It involves embracing our humanity, flaws and all, in a way that leads to greater self-compassion and spiritual clarity. Through this practice, we can understand the deeper motivations behind our behaviors, reactions, and choices, ultimately guiding us toward a more fulfilling life.

Hidden Gifts:
Uncovering the Positive Power of the Shadow

When people first hear the term shadow work, they often assume it's about confronting the darkest, most negative parts of themselves. While shadow work does involve facing difficult aspects, it's not just about our fears, anger, or shame. Many positive qualities—courage, creativity, assertiveness, and passion—can also be found within the shadow. Often, these traits are hidden because they've been misunderstood, neglected, or even suppressed by our upbringing or society's expectations. This chapter is a journey into discovering and reclaiming these "hidden gifts" of the shadow, showing us that shadow work is a path not only to self- acceptance but also to greater inner strength and potential.

The Golden Shadow:
Recognizing Our Hidden Strengths

Psychologists often talk about the golden shadow—the positive aspects of ourselves that we fail to see or accept. Just as we bury traits we dislike, we also hide away strengths and talents that we're afraid to express, perhaps out of fear of standing out, being judged, or even feeling unworthy of them. These hidden strengths may include:

- **Creativity:** Sometimes we suppress creativity because it feels impractical or we fear criticism. Yet, within the shadow, this creativity quietly waits for expression, and reclaiming it can bring us immense joy and fulfillment.

- **Self-Confidence:** If we've been taught to stay humble or avoid taking up space, our confidence may become part of the shadow. When we reclaim it, we allow ourselves to shine without guilt or shame.

- **Assertiveness:** Many people fear being assertive because they associate it with aggression. But assertiveness is simply the ability to express our needs clearly. When we reclaim it, we feel empowered to stand up for ourselves and others.

By exploring these hidden traits, we come to see that the shadow is not something to fear. Instead, it's a treasure chest of qualities that, when embraced, lead us to a fuller, more authentic self.

When Shadows Eclipse Our Light: Barriers to Growth and Spiritual Awakening

Though we may believe we can suppress our shadows, they often manifest in subtle and disruptive ways. Unresolved aspects of ourselves can lead to destructive patterns, such as self- sabotage, relationship issues, or feelings of unworthiness. These shadows may fuel feelings of shame, bitterness, or even unconscious resentments that weigh down our emotional and spiritual well-being.

Spiritually, shadows act as barriers between us and the divine. The Bible often speaks of removing obstacles that keep us from a closer relationship with God, and in many cases, these obstacles are the shadows we refuse to acknowledge. When left unchecked, they limit our capacity for personal growth, peace, and spiritual insight. To grow in our faith and spiritual journey, we must face these shadows, allowing the light of understanding and grace to dissolve them.

How to Overcome Our Shadows

Overcoming our shadows requires a gentle, intentional approach. While shadow work can be challenging, it is also deeply rewarding. We'll delve deeper into the process in Chapter 10, **How to Overcome Our Shadows**, but here's a straightforward guide to get you started:

1. Acknowledge the Existence of the Shadow

The first step is recognizing that the shadow exists. Reflect on recurring patterns in your life— moments of intense emotion, repeated mistakes, or uncomfortable reactions. These are often clues pointing to unresolved aspects of your inner self. Just as the Bible teaches self-examination, this is an opportunity to humbly look within and admit what you've been avoiding.

2. Cultivate Self-Compassion

Before delving into deeper layers of shadow work, it's crucial to approach yourself with compassion. Often, our shadows are linked to pain or difficult experiences from our past. Just as God's grace is extended to us, we must learn to extend grace to ourselves. Embrace the idea that no one is perfect, and imperfections are part of the human experience.

3. Identify the Specific Shadows

Spend time identifying what specific aspects of yourself you've been repressing. This could be anger, fear, guilt, or a sense of inadequacy. Journaling can be a helpful tool during this step. Ask yourself: "What emotions or behaviors do I feel ashamed of? Where in my life do I feel stuck or frustrated?" Be honest and open with what arises.

4. Reflect on the Origin

Once you've identified a shadow, reflect on its origin. Shadows are often formed early in life, through painful experiences, trauma, or learned behaviors. Ask yourself: "When did I first start feeling this way? What happened that led me to suppress this part of myself?" Understanding the root of a shadow can be profoundly liberating.

5. Bring the Shadow into the Light

To integrate the shadow, you must consciously bring it into the light of awareness. This step is about acknowledging your shadow without judgment, offering it a space to exist within you. Just as biblical figures like David and Jacob confronted their flaws, we must face our shadows with courage and honesty. It's through this confrontation that transformation occurs.

6. Transform the Shadow into Growth

The final step is to transform your shadow into an opportunity for growth. Once you've identified, accepted, and understood your shadow, ask yourself: "What can this teach me? How can I grow from this?" In biblical terms, this is a moment of redemption—taking what was once seen as a weakness or flaw and turning it into a strength or a lesson for the future.

Implementing the Biblical Tarot in Shadow Work

The Biblical Tarot: Shadows of the Soul was created as a powerful tool to guide you through the process of shadow work by drawing on the wisdom of the Bible. Here's how you can incorporate the deck into your shadow work practice:

Use the Cards for Reflection

Each card in the deck represents a biblical story or character, which mirrors the internal struggles we face in our lives. Begin your shadow work session by selecting a card. Reflect on the story or figure depicted on the card and consider how it relates to your current shadow work. For instance, the story of Jacob wrestling with God might speak to an inner conflict you're currently facing, symbolizing the struggle to accept a part of yourself.

Meditate on the Card's Message

After selecting a card, spend time meditating on its message. How does the biblical story align with your current emotional state or personal challenge? Ask yourself: "What is God trying to teach me through this story? How does this card help me better understand my shadow?"

Journal Your Reflections

Writing down your thoughts can be a powerful way to process your emotions and insights. Use a journal to record your reflections on the card, the shadow it represents, and the lessons you're learning. This act of documenting your journey mirrors the biblical tradition of recording spiritual insights and struggles.

Pray for Guidance and Strength

Prayer can be an essential part of integrating the lessons of shadow work. Ask God for the courage to face your shadows, the wisdom to understand their meaning, and the strength to transform them. Lean on your faith throughout the process, trusting that God is guiding you toward healing and growth.

Shadow work, when done with intention and grace, offers the opportunity for profound spiritual transformation. The Biblical Tarot: Shadows of the Soul is not merely a tool for self-reflection; it is a companion on the journey toward spiritual wholeness, illuminating the path toward greater self-awareness and divine connection.

Chapter 9

The Collective Shadow

– Healing Self, Healing Society

Shadow work is often seen as an inward journey, a process of facing personal fears, desires, and hidden parts of the self. Yet, our individual shadows don't exist in isolation. Each of us is influenced by societal norms, cultural beliefs, and shared values, many of which have developed over generations. This layer of shared unconscious beliefs is known as the collective shadow— the hidden and denied aspects of humanity that shape our societies, institutions, and individual psyches. Understanding the collective shadow gives us a broader perspective on shadow work, helping us see how our personal challenges are often reflections of societal dynamics. This chapter explores the concept of the collective shadow and its role in individual growth, healing, and contribution to the collective good.

Defining the Collective Shadow

In Jungian psychology, the collective unconscious is the shared reservoir of memories, instincts, and archetypes common to all humans.

Within this collective unconscious lies the collective shadow—aspects of human nature that society prefers to ignore or deny. These may include cultural prejudices, stigmas, unresolved historical trauma, and unexamined societal values. The collective shadow is made up of qualities that a society suppresses, whether out of fear, taboo, or because they clash with cultural ideals. These shadows don't disappear; instead, they linger in the subconscious, subtly influencing individuals' beliefs, actions, and perceptions.

By understanding the collective shadow, we gain insight into how cultural conditioning impacts our personal shadow. Recognizing these influences enables us to release beliefs and behaviors that may be rooted more in societal expectations than in our authentic selves, allowing us to approach shadow work with a clearer, more compassionate perspective.

How the Collective Shadow Influences Personal Shadows

Our personal shadows often form as a response to cultural norms and expectations. Societies and cultures, much like individuals, have qualities they idealize and traits they suppress. For example, many cultures celebrate strength and independence while discouraging vulnerability, emotion, or rest. As individuals growing up within these frameworks, we may internalize these values, repressing our own "unacceptable" traits to fit societal ideals. Over time, these repressed qualities become part of our personal shadow, creating conflicts and challenges that can remain hidden if not consciously examined.

In shadow work, recognizing the influence of the collective shadow allows us to question which parts of our shadow are authentically ours and which are societal expectations we've unconsciously internalized. For instance, we might ask ourselves: "Is this fear of failure truly mine, or is it something society has instilled in me?" This exploration allows us to release beliefs that don't align with our true self, moving us toward a more liberated and authentic identity.

Examples of the Collective Shadow in Society

The collective shadow manifests in various societal norms and beliefs, often creating unspoken pressure to conform. Some common examples include:

- **Stigmas around Vulnerability:** Many cultures glorify strength and self-sufficiency, which can lead to the repression of emotions perceived as "weak," such as sadness, fear, or dependence. This creates a collective shadow that labels vulnerability as undesirable.

- **Material Success as Self-Worth:** Societies that prioritize productivity and material wealth often push individuals to equate their worth with their achievements. Qualities like rest, creativity, or compassion may become shadows, as they are seen as less valuable.

- **Gender Norms and Expectations:** Societal expectations around masculinity and femininity often cause individuals to repress qualities that don't align with these norms. For instance, sensitivity in men and assertiveness in women may become part of their shadow, creating inner conflicts.

By exploring these collective shadows, we start to see how much of what we struggle with individually reflects larger social pressures. This awareness allows us to separate our true selves from these inherited beliefs, making space for authentic growth.

The Role of the Collective Shadow in Family and Ancestral Influences

The collective shadow doesn't just influence individuals on a societal level; it also manifests in family beliefs and generational patterns. Families often pass down values, fears, and judgments that are part of the broader cultural context. This inheritance may include fears around security, success, or self-expression, which children internalize without question. These family patterns shape our personal shadow, and without conscious examination, they often repeat from generation to generation.

For example, a family that grew up during hardship may unconsciously pass down scarcity mindsets, instilling fears about security, finances, or even trusting others. When we engage in shadow work, we have the opportunity to break these inherited patterns, freeing ourselves and future generations from unhelpful conditioning. Understanding how the collective shadow affects family dynamics empowers us to approach shadow work with compassion, breaking cycles and embracing beliefs aligned with our true values.

The Collective Shadow and Societal Crises

The collective shadow often surfaces during times of societal crises, such as economic downturns, political unrest, or social inequality. These events force societies to confront deeply ingrained fears, biases, and conflicts. For instance, economic crises may expose fears around security, political conflicts may reveal collective power struggles, and social movements may confront prejudices that have long been ignored. In these moments, society as a whole is forced to acknowledge its shadows, just as individuals are in shadow work.

Understanding the collective shadow in the context of societal crises reminds us that our personal growth and healing have a ripple effect. By engaging in our own shadow work, we challenge collective patterns, helping to transform the beliefs and biases that perpetuate suffering. This interconnectedness underscores the value of individual healing for collective progress, as each person who engages in shadow work contributes to a more compassionate, inclusive society.

Archetypes and the Collective Shadow in Tarot

In the tarot, many archetypal cards represent aspects of the collective shadow. These archetypes highlight both personal and societal themes, allowing us to explore our inner dynamics within a larger framework.

The Devil: Reflects attachments, desires, and fears we share collectively. It can represent societal issues like addiction to material wealth or avoidance of self-reflection.

The Moon: Embodies the hidden and subconscious aspects of society, encouraging us to explore beliefs we may not fully understand or accept.

The Tower: Represents upheaval, both personal and collective. It's a call to break down false structures, whether in our personal lives or within society, paving the way for change.

When these cards appear in a reading, they invite us to examine the influence of the collective shadow on our personal lives. For example, drawing The Devil may prompt us to consider how much of our attachment to success or control is shaped by societal values. These archetypes offer a dual perspective, allowing us to see how our personal shadows are intertwined with collective dynamics.

Working with the Collective Shadow

To fully integrate our personal shadows, it's important to acknowledge the impact of the collective shadow. Here are practical steps to help readers work with both personal and collective shadows in their shadow work:

- **Identify Collective Beliefs You've Internalized:** Reflect on which traits you suppress and whether these repressed qualities are influenced by societal expectations. Ask questions like, "Is this belief truly mine, or is it something society values?"

- **Examine Family and Ancestral Patterns:** Reflect on values and fears passed down from your family. Are there generational beliefs about security, success, or self-worth that you've unconsciously accepted? Shadow work allows you to release patterns that don't align with your true self, breaking cycles for future generations.

- **Use Tarot to Reflect on Societal Influences:** Cards like The Devil, The Moon, and The Tower offer insights into the collective shadow. When these cards appear, consider how much of their message relates to personal issues versus societal expectations.

- **Journal on Cultural Norms and Personal Truths:** Write about the values your culture or society holds, and compare them to your personal beliefs. This practice clarifies which values resonate with you and which ones you may have outgrown or wish to release.

- **Practice Compassionate Reflection:** Remember that the collective shadow represents universal human experiences. Approaching it with compassion helps us let go of judgment, both for ourselves and for others, and fosters understanding that shadow aspects are a shared part of humanity.

Healing the Collective Through Personal Growth

Shadow work may seem like an individual journey, but it has a profound collective impact. Each person who engages in this process, confronting fears, biases, and limitations, contributes to healing the collective shadow. When we question societal norms, release inherited beliefs, and embrace authenticity, we influence those around us, helping to create a more compassionate and accepting world.

The collective shadow reminds us that our individual journey is part of a larger whole. By healing ourselves, we heal society. Each step toward personal understanding and wholeness has a ripple effect, challenging and transforming the collective beliefs that shape us all. This interconnectedness inspires us to engage in shadow work with a sense of purpose, knowing that the inner work we do contributes to a brighter, more inclusive collective future.

In exploring the collective shadow, we gain a fuller understanding of our personal shadow work journey. Recognizing the cultural, societal, and familial influences in our shadows helps us approach our inner work with compassion and perspective, creating space for both personal and collective healing. The journey to self-awareness is not just a path to individual growth—it's a way to uplift and transform the world around us.

Chapter 10

How to Overcome Our Shadows

The shadows we carry within us are not our enemies; they are fragments of ourselves longing to be seen, understood, and integrated. Overcoming these shadows is not about erasing them but about transforming them into sources of strength and wisdom. This chapter will guide you through the process of recognizing, confronting, and ultimately embracing the hidden aspects of your psyche. With patience and courage, you'll uncover the profound gifts that lie in the parts of yourself you've kept in the dark. This journey is not easy, but it is deeply rewarding—a path to wholeness, balance, and inner peace.

Acknowledge the Existence of the Shadow

The journey of shadow work begins with acknowledging that we all have shadows—parts of ourselves we'd rather not face. Many of us go through life unaware of these hidden aspects, but their effects show up in our thoughts, emotions, and behaviors. Often, our shadows manifest in repeated patterns of self-sabotage, fear, anger, or defensiveness. The key is recognizing these patterns and understanding that they stem from unexamined parts of ourselves.

Practical Ways to Acknowledge the Shadow:

- **Pay attention to triggers:** Notice what situations or people trigger strong emotional reactions in you. These reactions can serve as clues to the parts of yourself that you've been repressing.

- **Practice self-reflection:** Set aside time for daily or weekly self-reflection. Journal about your experiences, focusing on moments when you felt particularly upset or defensive. Ask yourself: "What was really happening inside me?"

- **Seek feedback:** Sometimes, our shadows are so deeply buried that we need help seeing them. Ask trusted friends or family members for honest feedback about recurring patterns they notice in you. While this can be uncomfortable, it can also be incredibly illuminating.

The Bible often speaks about self-examination and the importance of looking inward to uncover our sins and imperfections. Acknowledging the shadow is the first step toward spiritual and personal growth, allowing you to face the parts of yourself that have remained hidden.

Cultivate Self-Compassion

Shadow work can be an uncomfortable and humbling experience. As we start to uncover the hidden aspects of ourselves, we may feel ashamed or upset about what we find. That's why cultivating self-compassion is crucial. Just as God offers us grace, we must learn to offer that same grace to ourselves. Shadows are often formed as a result of pain, trauma, or difficult circumstances. By being kind to ourselves, we create a safe space in which healing can occur.

Practical Ways to Cultivate Self-Compassion:

- **Self-affirmations:** Start each day by affirming that you are worthy of love and growth. Remind yourself that it's okay to have flaws and that everyone has a shadow side.

- **Be mindful of self-criticism:** Notice when you're being harsh or critical with yourself. Replace judgmental thoughts with kind and understanding ones. Instead of saying, "I'm so bad for feeling this way," try, "It's okay that I'm feeling this; it's part of being human."

- **Practice forgiveness:** The Bible teaches us the importance of forgiveness, both for others and ourselves. When you uncover difficult aspects of your shadow, consciously practice forgiving yourself for past mistakes, just as you would forgive someone else.

Compassion helps create the emotional resilience needed for shadow work. Without it, we risk spiraling into self-criticism or avoidance, preventing us from fully engaging with the process.

Identify the Specific Shadows

This step is about shining a light on the specific traits, emotions, or behaviors that make up your shadow. It's important to take the time to identify these shadows so you can work on integrating them. Common shadows include jealousy, anger, fear, and guilt, but they can also manifest as suppressed desires, feelings of unworthiness, or tendencies toward manipulation or control.

Practical Ways to Identify Specific Shadows:

- **Keep a shadow journal:** Use a journal to document recurring emotions or behaviors that cause discomfort. Write down situations where you feel particularly vulnerable, defensive, or reactive. Ask yourself: "What part of myself am I hiding or suppressing in this moment?"

- **Notice projections:** Often, the traits we dislike in others are reflections of our own shadow. For example, if you find yourself irritated by someone's arrogance, consider whether this irritation reflects a part of yourself that you've repressed or denied.

- **Explore your fears and insecurities:** Shadows often hide behind our fears. Take some time to explore what you're most afraid of in life—fear of failure, fear of rejection, or fear of being unworthy. These fears can lead you to deeper insights about your shadow.

Identifying your shadows is essential because it gives you a clearer target for healing and transformation. Once you know what specific aspects need attention, you can begin working on them with greater intention.

Reflect on the Origin

Once you've identified a specific shadow, it's important to explore where it came from. Shadows often originate from childhood experiences, past traumas, or cultural conditioning.

Understanding the root cause of your shadow can provide valuable context and help you see why certain emotions or behaviors were repressed in the first place.

Practical Ways to Reflect on the Origin:

- **Think back to your childhood:** Many of our shadows are formed early in life, when we learn what behaviors or emotions are "acceptable" and which ones aren't. Reflect on your early relationships with family, friends, and authority figures. Were there emotions you were discouraged from expressing? Were certain behaviors frowned upon?

- **Examine your life experiences:** Trauma, loss, or difficult life events can lead to the formation of shadows. Ask yourself: "What major experiences have shaped my views of myself and others?" Consider whether unresolved pain from those experiences has contributed to your shadow.

- **Consult the biblical narrative:** The Bible is filled with stories of people wrestling with their inner darkness. Look to figures like David, who struggled with guilt and fear, or Moses, who confronted his doubts and insecurities. These stories can offer insight into how your shadow might have been shaped.

Understanding the origin of your shadow is a powerful step because it allows you to approach it with empathy and a sense of context. When you see your shadow as something that formed to protect or cope with past pain, it becomes easier to heal and integrate.

Bring the Shadow into the Light

Bringing the shadow into the light means consciously facing the parts of yourself that you've repressed. It's about accepting that these traits or emotions exist, rather than continuing to deny or suppress them. This step requires courage and vulnerability, as it involves confronting uncomfortable truths about yourself.

Practical Ways to Bring the Shadow into the Light:

- **Own your shadow:** Begin by acknowledging that your shadow is a part of who you are. Instead of rejecting or feeling ashamed of it, accept that it has been part of your journey. For example, if you've identified anger as part of your shadow, recognize that anger has been a way for you to express unmet needs or boundaries.

- **Practice transparency:** Be honest with yourself and others about your shadow. You don't need to reveal everything to everyone, but sharing your process with a trusted friend, family member, or therapist can be healing. Verbalizing your shadow helps diminish its power over you.

- **Use biblical stories as mirrors:** As you explore the stories of biblical figures who struggled with their own shadows—like Peter's denial of Jesus or Jonah's fear and avoidance—reflect on how their journeys mirror your own. What can you learn from their courage to face their flaws?

By bringing the shadow into the light, you start the process of integration. It's not about eliminating the shadow, but about making it a conscious part of your self-awareness, which leads to personal empowerment and growth.

Transform the Shadow into Growth

The final step in shadow work is transforming what was once hidden or repressed into an opportunity for growth. The Bible teaches that God brings beauty out of brokenness, and this is true for our shadows as well. By integrating the shadow, we can harness its energy in positive ways, turning weaknesses into strengths and limitations into opportunities for learning.

Practical Ways to Transform the Shadow into Growth:

- **Reframe your shadow:** Consider how your shadow, when integrated, can become a source of strength. For example, if you've repressed assertiveness, learning to embrace this trait could help you set healthier boundaries and stand up for yourself.

- **Set intentions for change:** After acknowledging and accepting your shadow, make conscious choices about how to move forward. Ask yourself: "How can I apply what I've learned about my shadow to my life?" This could mean setting new boundaries, expressing emotions more freely, or addressing unresolved pain with compassion.

- **Seek spiritual guidance:** Prayer, meditation, and reading Scripture can help you find clarity as you integrate your shadow. Ask God for the wisdom to use what you've learned for your spiritual and personal growth. Reflect on verses that speak to transformation, such as Romans 12:2: "Do not conform to the pattern of this world, but be transformed by the renewing of your mind."

Transformation is the ultimate goal of shadow work. By turning what was once hidden into a conscious source of growth, you allow yourself to live more authentically, align more closely with your values, and deepen your connection to the Divine.

Conclusion: Embracing the Journey

Overcoming our shadows is a lifelong journey, but it's one that leads to profound personal and spiritual transformation. By following these six steps—acknowledging, cultivating compassion, identifying, reflecting on origins, bringing the shadow into the light, and transforming it—you'll gain the tools you need to grow, heal, and live in greater alignment with your true self.

Chapter 11

Integration with Prayer and Meditation

Shadow work can be an intense and transformative process, often revealing parts of ourselves that we have long ignored or denied. Prayer offers a way to bring these revelations before God, asking for divine guidance, healing, and strength. Through prayer, we invite God into the shadow work process, trusting in His grace to lead us as we confront our hidden struggles.

Prayer is a tool for reflection, connection, and release. It allows us to surrender our burdens, invite God's wisdom, and remind ourselves of the grace that is always available to us. The Bible teaches that God sees all parts of us, even those parts we hide from ourselves, and yet we are still loved and accepted.

As you engage with shadow work, prayer can be a steady companion—a means of grounding yourself, seeking comfort, and finding clarity. It offers a direct line to divine support, helping you navigate the emotional and spiritual complexities of integrating your shadow.

How to Incorporate Prayer:

- **Start with Gratitude:** Begin each shadow work session by thanking God for the opportunity to grow. Acknowledge His presence in your journey and express gratitude for the grace that allows you to confront your shadow without fear.

  Example Prayer: "Lord, I thank You for this time of reflection and growth. I invite Your wisdom and grace into this moment as I seek to understand the hidden parts of myself."

- **Ask for Guidance:** As you draw a card or reflect on a specific aspect of your shadow, ask God for insight and understanding. Pray for the courage to face your shadow and for the clarity to discern what needs healing.

  Example Prayer: "God, I ask for Your guidance as I explore this shadow. Help me see with clarity and understanding. Give me the strength to face what is hidden, knowing that You are with me through every step."

- **Offer Up Your Shadow:** Once you've identified a shadow, surrender it to God through prayer. Acknowledge it without judgment and ask for divine help in integrating it. This practice of surrender can bring peace and acceptance.

  Example Prayer: "Father, I bring before You this part of myself that I've long denied. Help me to embrace it with compassion and to learn from it. Heal the wounds that have kept me in darkness and guide me toward wholeness."

- **Conclude with a Request for Transformation:** End your session by asking God to help transform your shadow into a source of growth. Remember that in biblical teachings, God brings beauty from brokenness and redemption from struggle.

Example Prayer: "Lord, I ask that You transform this shadow into a source of strength and wisdom. Help me grow in Your grace, learning from these hidden parts of myself, and becoming more aligned with Your purpose for my life."

Meditation on Scripture for Shadow Work

Biblical meditation can deepen the experience of shadow work by anchoring it in the timeless wisdom of Scripture. Meditation on God's Word helps create space for reflection, allowing insights from your shadow work to settle in your mind and heart.

In the Bible, meditation is often described as reflecting deeply on the Word of God, allowing it to permeate your thoughts and transform your perspective. Shadow work benefits from this practice because biblical teachings provide wisdom, encouragement, and reminders of God's grace.

When meditating on Scripture during shadow work, you can choose verses that speak to healing, transformation, self-examination, or God's unwavering love. These meditations help you frame your shadow work not just as a psychological journey, but as a spiritual practice deeply rooted in faith.

How to Incorporate Biblical Meditation:

- **Choose a Verse That Resonates with Your Shadow Work:** After reflecting on a tarot reading or journaling about a shadow, find a Scripture that connects with the emotions or insights that surfaced. For example:

  » If you're working through fear or self-doubt, meditate on Isaiah 41:10: "Fear not, for I am with you; be not dismayed, for I am your God. I will strengthen you, I will help you, I will uphold you with my righteous right hand."

  » If you're struggling with guilt or shame, reflect on Romans 8:1: "There is therefore now no condemnation for those who are in Christ Jesus."

- **Enter into Quiet Reflection:** Find a quiet space where you can sit in stillness with the chosen verse. Slowly repeat the Scripture to yourself, letting the words sink in. As you meditate, allow the message of the verse to interact with the shadow you've identified. What does the verse reveal about this hidden part of yourself? How does it speak to your healing process?

- **Ask for God's Wisdom:** As you meditate on the verse, invite God's wisdom into your reflection. You might ask: "What are You trying to teach me through this verse, Lord? How does this Scripture help me integrate what I've learned from my shadow work?"

- **Rest in the Message:** After meditating, spend a few moments resting in the message of the Scripture. Let it provide comfort, healing, or insight as you continue your shadow work journey.

Suggested Verses for Shadow Work:

- **Self-Examination:** Psalm 139:23-24 – "Search me, God, and know my heart; test me and know my anxious thoughts. See if there is any offensive way in me, and lead me in the way everlasting."

- **Healing and Transformation:** 2 Corinthians 5:17 – "Therefore, if anyone is in Christ, the new creation has come: The old has gone, the new is here!"

- **God's Grace in Struggles:** 2 Corinthians 12:9 – "But He said to me, 'My grace is sufficient for you, for My power is made perfect in weakness.' Therefore I will boast all the more gladly about my weaknesses, so that Christ's power may rest on me."

- **Overcoming Fear and Doubt:** Joshua 1:9 – "Have I not commanded you? Be strong and courageous. Do not be afraid; do not be discouraged, for the Lord your God will be with you wherever you go."

A Daily Practice:
Combining Prayer, Meditation, and Shadow Work

To create a regular practice of integrating prayer, meditation, and shadow work, consider the following daily routine:

- **Begin with Prayer:** Start by asking God to guide your shadow work and reveal what needs healing.

- **Pull a Card and Reflect:** Use your Biblical Tarot: Shadows of the Soul to draw a card and reflect on the story or figure it represents. Allow your subconscious to reveal any shadows connected to the card.

- **Journal Your Insights:** Write down your thoughts, emotions, and any shadows that surface during the reflection.

- **Meditate on Scripture:** Choose a verse related to your shadow and spend a few moments in quiet meditation, allowing the Word of God to bring clarity and comfort.

- **Conclude with Prayer:** Close your session by offering up your shadow to God, asking for healing and transformation.

Conclusion:
A Spiritual Practice of Reflection and Healing

By integrating prayer and meditation with your shadow work, you create a sacred space where spiritual and psychological healing can coexist. Prayer invites God's grace into the process, while meditation on Scripture grounds you in biblical wisdom, offering comfort and guidance as you explore your inner depths.

Through these practices, shadow work becomes more than just self-examination—it becomes a spiritual journey of redemption, transformation, and connection with the Divine. In this sacred space, you're not alone in facing your shadows. God walks with you, offering strength, wisdom, and healing at every step.

Chapter 12

The Role of Grace and Redemption

The Power of Grace in Shadow Work

At the heart of the Christian faith lies the concept of grace—God's unconditional love and favor, extended to us even when we feel undeserving. Grace is not something we earn; it is a gift freely given by God. In the context of shadow work, grace is essential. As we confront our inner darkness and hidden flaws, we often feel guilt, shame, or regret for the aspects of ourselves we've repressed. This is where grace becomes our anchor. It reminds us that, no matter how difficult or messy the process of shadow work may be, we are still loved and accepted by God.

Grace allows us to approach shadow work with humility rather than self-condemnation. Instead of seeing our shadows as failures or moral shortcomings, grace invites us to view them as opportunities for growth, healing, and transformation. It helps us see ourselves as God sees us— whole, loved, and constantly evolving.

Why Grace is Important:

- **Self-Compassion:** Without grace, shadow work can become an exercise in self-criticism. We might focus too much on our flaws and mistakes, leading to feelings of unworthiness. Grace allows us to extend compassion to ourselves, realizing that we are all imperfect and in need of divine love. Just as God forgives us, we must learn to forgive ourselves as we confront our shadows.

- **Freedom from Guilt:** Shadow work often brings up emotions tied to past mistakes, failures, or harmful behaviors. While it's important to acknowledge these aspects, grace offers freedom from the heavy burden of guilt. The Bible teaches us that through Christ, we are forgiven, and this forgiveness allows us to move forward without being trapped by our past.

- **Courage to Face the Shadow:** Grace gives us the courage to face our shadows honestly, knowing that we are not defined by our flaws. When we feel the weight of grace, we can approach our inner work with a sense of hope, trusting that transformation is possible. Grace empowers us to dive deep into the parts of ourselves that need healing, knowing we are not alone in the process.

The Role of Redemption in Shadow Work

Redemption is the process by which God transforms what is broken, sinful, or lost into something whole, beautiful, and purposeful. The Bible is filled with stories of redemption, from the forgiveness extended to the prodigal son to the transformation of Paul from persecutor to apostle. Redemption is not just about being forgiven for our sins—it's about allowing God to use our struggles and imperfections to create something greater.

In shadow work, redemption is the ultimate goal. As we uncover and confront our shadows, the aim is not to eradicate these parts of ourselves but to integrate and transform them. Through redemption, the traits or behaviors that once hindered us can become sources of strength, wisdom, and compassion.

Why Redemption is Important:

- **Turning Darkness into Light:** Shadow work can feel heavy because it involves confronting painful or uncomfortable parts of ourselves. But redemption reminds us that these very parts can be transformed into something positive. For example, someone who struggles with anger may, through shadow work, learn to channel that energy into setting healthy boundaries or advocating for justice. God's redemptive power turns our darkness into light.

- **Healing and Restoration:** Redemption is about healing what is broken. As we work through our shadows, we experience moments of restoration—where the aspects of ourselves that were once fragmented become whole again. This mirrors the biblical promise of redemption: "I will restore you to health and heal your wounds" (Jeremiah 30:17). Shadow work becomes not just a process of self-discovery, but one of divine healing.

- **Living with Purpose:** Once we have integrated and redeemed our shadows, we often find that the very things we struggled with can now serve a greater purpose in our lives. The Bible teaches us that God uses all things for good, even our struggles (Romans 8:28). As we redeem our shadows, we step into a fuller understanding of our purpose and potential.

Grace and Redemption:
A Spiritual Foundation for Shadow Work

Together, grace and redemption form the spiritual foundation for shadow work. Without grace, we might be overwhelmed by our shadows, feeling unworthy or stuck in self-judgment. Without redemption, we might believe that our shadows are simply negative aspects of ourselves, rather than opportunities for transformation.

As you walk through the process of shadow work, remember these truths:

- Grace frees you from guilt, shame, and fear. It allows you to approach your shadow work with love and compassion, knowing that you are fully accepted by God, no matter what you uncover.

- Redemption gives purpose to your shadows. It reminds you that the parts of yourself you've kept hidden are not to be erased but transformed. What was once broken can be made whole. What was once dark can be brought into the light.

When we allow grace and redemption to guide our shadow work, the process becomes not just an exploration of the self but a profound spiritual journey. It is a journey of becoming— becoming more aware of who we are, more aligned with our purpose, and more connected to the divine love that holds us through it all.

Conclusion:
Embracing the Gift of Transformation

In the end, shadow work is about transformation. Through grace, we learn to accept ourselves with all our flaws and imperfections. Through redemption, we allow God to use those imperfections for good. The shadows we once feared become sources of light, wisdom, and healing.

Grace and redemption remind us that we are never defined by our shadows. Instead, we are constantly being transformed by the love of God, moving toward wholeness and purpose. Embrace this journey with an open heart, trusting that every shadow holds the potential for growth, and every flaw can be redeemed in the hands of the Divine.

Chapter 13

Rituals and Practices
for Grounding

The Importance of Grounding in Shadow Work

Shadow work can stir up deep emotions, past traumas, and unac-knowledged fears. As we confront these hidden aspects of ourselves, it's normal to feel unsettled, overwhelmed, or even vulnerable. This is where grounding practices come in. Grounding is the act of connect-ing yourself to the present moment and finding stability amidst the emotional turbulence that can accompany inner work. These rituals or practices help you remain centered and calm, allowing you to process what emerges from your shadow work without becoming overwhelmed.

The Bible speaks of God as our foundation, a rock on which we can rely in times of uncertainty and challenge. Grounding practices serve a similar role—they provide a stable foundation when you're exploring the deeper, hidden parts of yourself. They help you maintain balance, calm your nervous system, and create a sense of safety as you work through your shadows.

Incorporating grounding rituals into your shadow work routine can also help prevent burnout or emotional fatigue, ensuring that you approach this journey with patience, care, and gentleness.

Grounding Practices to Support Shadow Work

Below are several simple grounding rituals and practices that you can incorporate into your shadow work routine. Each practice is designed to help you reconnect with your body, the present moment, and the safety of God's presence as you explore your inner world.

Deep Breathing

Breathing is one of the simplest yet most effective grounding practices. When we're emotionally overwhelmed, our breathing often becomes shallow and rapid. Deep, slow breathing activates the body's parasympathetic nervous system, helping to calm both the mind and body.

How to Practice Deep Breathing:

- **Find a quiet space:** Sit comfortably and close your eyes.

- **Inhale deeply:** Breathe in through your nose for a count of four, letting your lungs fill fully.

- **Hold the breath:** Hold the breath gently for a count of four.

- **Exhale slowly:** Breathe out through your mouth for a count of six, releasing tension as you exhale.

- **Repeat:** Continue this cycle for 5-10 minutes, allowing each breath to ground you in the present moment.

Connecting with Nature

Nature has a calming and grounding effect on the mind and body. Spending time outdoors, even if only for a few minutes, can help you reconnect with the earth and bring a sense of peace and stability during intense shadow work. The Bible often speaks of nature as a reflection of God's presence and handiwork, making it a powerful tool for grounding.

How to Connect with Nature:

- **Take a mindful walk:** Walk outside, paying close attention to the sights, sounds, and sensations around you. Notice the rustling of leaves, the warmth of the sun, or the feeling of the ground beneath your feet.

- **Sit by a tree or body of water:** If possible, sit quietly in nature—by a tree, a river, or a garden. As you sit, imagine yourself becoming rooted to the earth, like a tree, grounded and stable. Let the stillness of nature calm your mind and spirit.

- **Bring nature indoors:** If you can't spend time outside, bring nature into your space. Place plants, stones, or natural objects around your home to create a grounding environment that connects you with the earth's energy.

Grounding Prayer or Affirmation

Prayer is a powerful grounding tool that reconnects you with God's presence, reminding you that you are not alone in your shadow work. A grounding prayer helps you center your thoughts, release fear, and place your trust in God's guidance.

Example Grounding Prayer: "Lord, as I enter this time of reflection, I ask You to ground me in Your love and presence. Help me stay present, open, and connected as I face the hidden parts of myself. Let Your peace calm my heart and guide my spirit. I trust in Your wisdom and grace to lead me through this journey. Amen."

Alternatively, you can use grounding affirmations that remind you of your inner strength and stability:

- "I am safe and grounded in this moment."

- "God's love is my foundation; I am steady and calm."

- "I release fear and trust in God's guidance."

Repeat these affirmations as needed to center yourself before or during shadow work sessions.

Body Awareness Meditation

Grounding involves reconnecting with your body, which can be particularly helpful when shadow work pulls you into deep or overwhelming emotions. A body awareness meditation helps bring your attention back to the physical world, anchoring you in the present moment.

How to Practice Body Awareness Meditation:

- **Sit or lie down comfortably:** Close your eyes and take a few deep breaths.

- **Scan your body:** Slowly bring your attention to different parts of your body, starting with your feet and working upward. Notice the sensations in each area—warmth, tension, heaviness, or lightness.

- **Breathe into each area:** As you focus on each body part, imagine sending your breath into that space, releasing any tension or discomfort.

- **Ground through your feet:** Finish by focusing on your feet, feeling them firmly on the ground. Imagine roots extending from your feet deep into the earth, anchoring you in place.

This practice helps you remain present in your body, releasing the emotional intensity of shadow work into the earth, where it can be absorbed and transformed.

Journaling to Ground Your Thoughts

Writing is a form of emotional release and grounding that allows you to process what emerges during shadow work. By putting your thoughts and feelings on paper, you create a sense of clarity and order, helping you to feel more grounded and less overwhelmed.

How to Practice Grounding Journaling:

- **Set a timer:** Dedicate 10-15 minutes to writing about your shadow work session. Don't worry about structure—just let your thoughts flow freely.

- **Release emotions onto the page:** Write about any emotions or insights that surfaced. Acknowledge how you're feeling, and allow yourself to release these thoughts onto the paper.

- **End with gratitude:** After journaling, take a moment to write down a few things you're grateful for, focusing on the present moment and the support available to you.

A Daily Grounding Ritual for Shadow Work

To create a routine that balances shadow work with grounding practices, consider the following daily ritual:

- **Begin with a Grounding Prayer:** Start with a prayer or affirmation to center your thoughts and ask for God's presence.

- **Pull a Tarot Card for Reflection:** Draw a card from the Biblical Tarot: Shadows of the Soul and reflect on the story or figure it represents. Let the card guide your exploration of any shadows that need attention.

- **Journal Your Insights:** Spend a few moments writing down your reflections and emotions.

- **Practice a Grounding Meditation or Breathing Exercise:** After journaling, engage in a short meditation, deep breathing, or body scan to reconnect with the present moment and release any emotional tension.

- **End with Gratitude:** Conclude your session by thanking God for His guidance and support, and take a moment to appreciate the grounding tools that help you stay centered.

Conclusion:
Grounding as a Spiritual Practice

Grounding rituals are not just tools for emotional regulation—they are spiritual practices that help you stay connected to yourself, to the earth, and to God. As you engage in shadow work, grounding offers a way to remain steady, present, and open to transformation. These simple practices help you navigate the emotional intensity of inner work while reminding you of the safety and stability provided by God's love.

In times of turbulence, remember that grounding is your way of returning to the present moment, finding peace, and trusting in God's grace. These practices will carry you through the depths of shadow work, ensuring that you remain centered, calm, and connected every step of the way.

Chapter 14

Discernment:

The Key to Wise Interpretation of Shadow Work Insights

The Role of Discernment in Shadow Work

As you engage in shadow work, you'll uncover many hidden aspects of yourself—emotions, memories, fears, and desires that have been buried deep in your subconscious. While it's empowering to bring these shadows to the surface, it's equally important to interpret what you uncover with wisdom and discernment. Discernment helps you navigate the complexities of shadow work, ensuring that you don't get lost in the emotions or thoughts that arise, but instead, gain clarity and understanding.

In the Bible, discernment is often spoken of as the ability to judge rightly, to distinguish between truth and falsehood, and to seek God's wisdom in navigating life's challenges. Proverbs 2:6 reminds us, "For the Lord gives wisdom; from His mouth come knowledge and understanding." In the context of shadow work, discernment allows you to sift through the emotions, insights, and reflections that arise, helping you determine what is true, what requires deeper exploration, and how to apply these insights to your life in a meaningful way.

Without discernment, there is a risk of misinterpreting your shadow work insights, either by over-identifying with certain emotions or becoming overwhelmed by the intensity of what you uncover. Discernment keeps you grounded, ensuring that your shadow work leads to growth, rather than confusion or despair.

How to Practice Discernment in Shadow Work

Below are key steps and tools to help you practice discernment as you interpret your shadow work insights:

- **Pause and Reflect Before Reacting:**
  When you uncover a hidden part of yourself, it's natural to feel a rush of emotions—whether it's anger, sadness, fear, or guilt. The first step in practicing discernment is to pause and reflect before reacting to these emotions. Allow yourself to sit with the insights for a moment, without jumping to conclusions or judgments about what they mean.

  » **Reflection Questions:**

  » What emotions am I feeling in this moment?

  » What is this shadow revealing about my inner world?

  » Is this insight tied to a specific event or belief from my past?

  By taking the time to reflect, you allow your emotions to settle, making it easier to interpret the meaning of the insight with clarity rather than emotional intensity.

- **Seek God's Guidance Through Prayer:**
  Discernment is often strengthened through prayer. When

you feel uncertain or confused about what a shadow is revealing, take a moment to seek God's wisdom. Ask for clarity, guidance, and the ability to interpret your insights in a way that aligns with God's will for your life.

> » **Example Prayer for Discernment:** "Lord, I come before You with this insight from my shadow work. I ask for Your wisdom and guidance to help me understand what this revelation means. Show me the truth behind my emotions and thoughts, and guide me on the path of healing and growth. Amen."

Turning to prayer helps you approach your shadow work with a spirit of humility and trust, knowing that God's wisdom can provide clarity in moments of uncertainty.

- **Look for Patterns and Repeated Themes:**
Discernment often comes from recognizing patterns or recurring themes in your shadow work. If certain emotions, fears, or beliefs surface repeatedly, they may point to deeper issues that require further exploration. Pay attention to insights that arise multiple times, as they may hold significant meaning for your growth.

> » **Reflection Questions:**

> » What patterns am I noticing in my shadow work?

> » Do certain emotions or beliefs keep coming up in different situations?

> » How do these patterns connect to my past experiences or unresolved issues?

By identifying patterns, you can discern which shadows are calling for more attention and which insights are key to your healing process.

- **Use Scripture as a Guide:**
  The Bible is a powerful tool for discernment, offering wisdom and guidance on how to navigate life's challenges, including the hidden aspects of ourselves. As you uncover insights from your shadow work, reflect on how these insights align with biblical teachings. Scripture can provide clarity, comfort, and direction as you work through difficult emotions or unresolved parts of your shadow.

  » **Reflection Questions:**

  » What does the Bible say about this emotion, behavior, or belief?

  » How can biblical teachings guide me in understanding this shadow?

  » Is there a particular Scripture that speaks to what I'm experiencing?

  By grounding your shadow work in Scripture, you can gain spiritual insight that helps you discern the truth behind your emotions and guide you toward a path of healing.

- **Journal Your Insights and Revisit Them Later:**
  Discernment often deepens with time. When you uncover a shadow or gain a new insight, write it down in a journal. After some time has passed, revisit your journal entries to see if new layers of understanding emerge. Sometimes, the meaning of a shadow or insight becomes clearer with distance, and what seemed confusing or overwhelming at first may reveal deeper wisdom when viewed from a fresh perspective.

  » **Reflection Practice:**

  » Write down your initial thoughts and emotions after a shadow work session.

» Return to your journal entry a week or month later to see if your understanding of the insight has changed or deepened.

» Reflect on any new perspectives or connections you've made since your original entry. Journaling helps you document your journey, making it easier to track your growth and discern the true meaning of your insights over time.

- **Seek Counsel from Trusted Mentors or Friends:** Discernment can also be strengthened through conversation with others. Sometimes, we are too close to our own shadows to see them clearly, and the perspective of a trusted mentor, spiritual advisor, or close friend can provide valuable insight. Sharing your shadow work journey with someone who understands the process can help you discern whether your interpretations are accurate and aligned with your personal and spiritual growth.

  » **How to Seek Support:**

  » Share your shadow work insights with a trusted person who has experience with inner work or spiritual guidance.

  » Ask for feedback or reflections on how they interpret the insights you've gained.

  » Be open to their perspectives, even if they challenge your initial interpretations. Receiving feedback from others can provide clarity, especially when emotions or complex shadows are clouding your judgment.

Avoiding Pitfalls in Interpretation

While discernment is about seeking clarity, it's also important to recognize potential pitfalls in the interpretation process. Below are a few common mistakes to avoid:

- **Over-Identifying with Shadows:**
  One common mistake is over-identifying with the shadow you uncover, believing that the hidden part of yourself defines you entirely. While your shadows are part of who you are, they do not represent the whole of your being. Discernment helps you maintain balance by reminding you that shadow work is about integration, not self-condemnation.

- **Rushing to Fix or Solve the Shadow:**
  It can be tempting to rush through shadow work in an effort to "fix" or "solve" the issue. However, shadow work is a gradual process of exploration and healing. Discernment encourages patience, allowing you to sit with your insights and learn from them, rather than rushing to a solution.

- **Ignoring Positive Aspects of the Shadow:**
  Shadows often contain both negative and positive traits. For example, someone who struggles with assertiveness may have suppressed their strength or leadership qualities. Discernment allows you to see both sides of the shadow—the part that needs healing and the part that can be transformed into a source of strength.

Conclusion:
Discerning with Wisdom and Grace

Discernment is an essential tool in shadow work, helping you wisely interpret the insights that emerge during your journey. By pausing to reflect, seeking God's guidance, recognizing patterns, and using Scripture as a guide, you can gain clarity about the deeper meaning of your shadows. With discernment, you are better equipped to navigate the complexities of your inner world, ensuring that your shadow work leads to healing, transformation, and spiritual growth.

As you continue your shadow work journey, remember that discernment is not about judging or condemning yourself—it is about seeking truth, understanding, and wisdom as you uncover and integrate the hidden parts of your soul.

Chapter 15

The Power of Community in Shadow Work

Shadow Work as a Personal and Collective Journey

Shadow work is often seen as a solitary journey, a deeply personal process of confronting hidden aspects of the self. And while the introspective nature of shadow work is essential, there is immense power in sharing this journey with others. The Bible teaches that we are not meant to walk the path of transformation alone. "As iron sharpens iron, so one person sharpens another" (Proverbs 27:17). This verse highlights the importance of community and mutual support in our spiritual and personal development.

Engaging in shadow work within a community can provide additional insights, emotional support, and accountability. When we feel supported, we are more likely to confront difficult truths, explore our shadows with courage, and grow through the process. Moreover, listening to others' experiences can mirror our own, offering perspectives we might not have considered.

By sharing our shadow work with trusted individuals or small groups, we create an environment where healing is not just an internal process but a communal one. In this chapter, we will explore how community can play a crucial role in shadow work and how the support of others can amplify our journey toward self-awareness and spiritual growth.

Why Community Support is Important in Shadow Work

While shadow work is intensely personal, bringing community into the process can enrich the experience in the following ways:

- **Accountability and Encouragement:**
  Shadow work requires courage and persistence, especially when we uncover parts of ourselves we've long suppressed. Having a community offers a sense of accountability, encouraging you to stay committed to the process even when it feels uncomfortable. Others can help you see patterns you may overlook and encourage you to continue exploring deeper layers of your shadow.

  When you share your progress or struggles with a supportive group, you receive encouragement to keep going, especially when the process feels overwhelming. Having someone check in on your progress or offer a word of support can make all the difference in sustaining the momentum of shadow work.

- **Sharing Insights and Perspectives:**
  One of the most powerful aspects of community is the exchange of perspectives. Others' experiences with their own shadows can provide valuable insights into your own process. As you hear stories of how others confront and integrate their shadows, you may recognize parallels

in your own life or discover new approaches to healing. In a community, collective wisdom is built through shared experiences. Listening to how others have navigated similar struggles allows you to learn from their journey, expanding your understanding of your own shadow and offering new tools for growth.

- **Validation and Empathy:**
  Shadow work can sometimes bring up feelings of guilt, shame, or fear. In a safe and supportive community, you can express these emotions without judgment, receiving validation for your experiences. When others respond with empathy and understanding, it reminds you that you are not alone in your struggles.

  Hearing someone say, "I've been there too" or "I understand what you're going through" can be incredibly comforting, especially when you're processing difficult emotions. This shared empathy reinforces that shadow work is a common human experience, not something to be ashamed of.

- **A Space for Reflection and Mirroring:**
  Communities offer an opportunity for mirroring—where others reflect back what they observe about you, helping you see aspects of your shadow that may be hidden from your own awareness. Others can provide honest, compassionate feedback about patterns they notice in your words, behaviors, or reactions. This mirroring helps you recognize blind spots, areas where your shadow may be influencing you in ways you haven't yet acknowledged.

In the context of shadow work, having others reflect on your progress or struggles helps you gain a clearer, more objective view of your inner journey. This can accelerate the process of self- awareness and deepen your understanding of the shadows you are working to integrate.

How to Find or Create a Supportive Community for Shadow Work

Not all spaces are conducive to shadow work. It's important to find or create a community that fosters trust, vulnerability, and mutual respect. Below are a few suggestions for finding or building a supportive environment for your shadow work journey:

- **Small, Trusted Circles:**
  Start by sharing your shadow work with a small circle of trusted individuals—people you know well and who will honor the vulnerability of this process. These might include close friends, spiritual mentors, or family members who understand the importance of self-reflection and growth.

  How to Start: Invite one or two people to join you in regular conversations or check-ins about your shadow work. Set clear intentions for the space, emphasizing that it is a non-judgmental and supportive environment. You can meet once a week or biweekly to discuss insights, challenges, and breakthroughs.

- **Shadow Work Support Groups:**
  If you don't already have a circle of people with whom you feel comfortable sharing your shadow work, consider joining or starting a shadow work support group. These groups can be in- person or virtual, and they provide a space where people can come together to explore shadow work in a guided and structured way.

  How to Start: Look for local or online communities dedicated to personal growth, spirituality, or inner work. Many groups focus on healing, self-discovery, or spiritual development, which can provide a supportive framework for shadow work. If no such group exists, you could create your own by gathering like-minded individuals and setting a shared intention for regular meetings focused on shadow work.

- **Partnering with a Spiritual Mentor or Counselor:**
  A spiritual mentor, counselor, or therapist trained in shadow work can provide invaluable support during the process. These individuals can offer guidance, ask insightful questions, and help you navigate difficult emotions that arise during shadow work.

  How to Start: If you feel comfortable, speak with a spiritual leader in your community about shadow work, or seek out a counselor who is familiar with both psychological and spiritual approaches to healing. Working one-on-one with someone who has experience in shadow work can accelerate your journey and provide a deeper level of support.

- **Study Groups for the Biblical Tarot:**
  One unique way to incorporate community into your shadow work is by creating a study group centered around the Biblical Tarot: Shadows of the Soul. In this setting, a small group could gather regularly to draw cards, reflect on their meaning, and share how each biblical story relates to their shadow work. This type of gathering can provide a supportive and spiritual framework for exploring the shadows.

  How to Start: Invite friends or community members to join you in a Bible-based tarot study group, where each session focuses on drawing cards and reflecting on their significance. The group can discuss the lessons of the cards, share personal insights, and offer support to one another as they journey through shadow work.

How to Share Your Shadow Work in Community

If you've never shared your shadow work journey with others, it can feel intimidating at first. The following steps can help you ease into the process and create meaningful conversations around shadow work:

- **Share in Small Doses:**
  You don't have to reveal everything at once. Start by sharing small pieces of your journey—an insight you gained from a tarot reading or a shadow you've been working on. As you feel more comfortable, you can open up about deeper emotions and more complex parts of your shadow work.

- **Focus on the Process, Not the Outcome:**
  When sharing your shadow work with others, it's important to focus on the process, rather than feeling like you have to "solve" or "fix" your shadow immediately. Let your community be a space for reflection, not perfection. Shadow work is a journey, and sharing that journey with others is just as valuable as achieving a particular outcome.

- **Listen with Compassion and Openness:**
  As important as it is to share, it's equally valuable to listen to others in the community. Approach their experiences with compassion, recognizing that everyone's shadow work journey is unique. Offer support and encouragement, and avoid judgment or unsolicited advice. Often, simply holding space for someone else to share their experience is the most helpful thing you can do.

Conclusion:
Walking the Journey Together

Shadow work is often seen as a solo endeavor, but the support of community can provide strength, insight, and encouragement when the journey feels challenging. Through the safety of trusted relationships, shared reflections, and compassionate feedback, community becomes a powerful ally in the process of integrating your shadow.

In the Bible, we see countless examples of the importance of community support—whether it's the disciples supporting one another in their faith or the early church gathering in unity to face challenges. In the same way, your shadow work can be enriched by the presence of others who are walking their own path of self-discovery and growth.

By embracing the power of community, you allow yourself to be seen, supported, and strengthened, knowing that the journey of shadow work is one that can be shared with others as you walk toward greater wholeness and spiritual connection.

Chapter 16

Belief Systems and Shadow Work

– Uncovering the Foundations of the Self

Beliefs are the silent architects of our lives, shaping how we see ourselves, interact with others, and respond to the world. These deeply held ideas can either empower us to grow and thrive or limit our potential, keeping us trapped in patterns of fear, doubt, or shame. For those engaging in shadow work, examining belief systems is a vital step toward understanding and integrating the hidden parts of the self.

In this chapter, we'll explore how beliefs influence our lives, their connection to the subconscious and the shadow, and how the Biblical Tarot: Shadows of the Soul can be used as a tool for uncovering and transforming belief systems.

What Are Belief Systems?

A belief system is a collection of principles, values, and ideas that govern how we interpret the world and our place within it. These beliefs can be conscious—statements we actively think and repeat—or unconscious, operating beneath the surface yet influencing every aspect of our behavior and emotions.

Beliefs often develop early in life, shaped by family, culture, religion, and personal experiences. Over time, they become filters through which we view ourselves and others, acting as guidelines for what we consider possible, acceptable, or true. While some beliefs support our growth and well-being, others may limit us, creating inner conflict and contributing to the shadow.

How Beliefs Influence Our Lives

Beliefs are like lenses that color every aspect of our lives. They affect how we approach relationships, challenges, and opportunities, influencing our actions and self-perception. Depending on whether they are empowering or limiting, beliefs can either uplift or hinder us.

- **Positive Beliefs:**

  Empowering beliefs, such as "I am capable of learning and growing" or "I deserve love and respect," provide a foundation for confidence, resilience, and emotional well-being.

  These beliefs encourage self-expression, creativity, and the courage to face challenges, fostering a mindset of abundance and possibility.

- **Negative Beliefs:**

  Limiting beliefs, such as "I am not good enough" or "Success is only for others," create barriers to growth and fulfillment. These beliefs often lead to self-sabotage, fear of failure, or a sense of unworthiness.

  Negative beliefs can reinforce the shadow, keeping repressed fears, insecurities, and emotions locked away, where they continue to influence behavior unconsciously.

For example, someone who believes "Anger is bad" may suppress their anger, causing it to build up and manifest in unhealthy ways, such as passive aggression or physical stress. By identifying and challenging such beliefs, shadow work helps to release these suppressed emotions and create healthier, more balanced ways of being.

Beliefs and the Subconscious

Many beliefs operate within the subconscious mind, the part of the psyche that lies below conscious awareness. This connection between beliefs and the subconscious is crucial in shadow work, as the subconscious is also where the shadow resides. When we internalize societal norms, cultural expectations, or family values, they often sink into the subconscious, becoming invisible yet powerful forces that guide our thoughts and actions.

For instance:

- A child raised in a family that values perfectionism may internalize the belief "I must be perfect to be loved." This belief, once embedded in the subconscious, shapes their behavior for years, even if they are no longer consciously aware of it.

- Similarly, cultural messages about gender roles or success may create subconscious beliefs that limit self-expression, such as "Vulnerability is weakness" or "Creativity is not practical."

By bringing these subconscious beliefs to light, shadow work allows us to question their validity and replace them with ones that align with our authentic selves.

Beliefs and the Shadow

Our beliefs determine what we accept about ourselves and what we suppress into the shadow. Traits or emotions that clash with our beliefs often become part of the shadow self, hidden from conscious awareness but influencing our behavior in subtle and sometimes destructive ways.

For example:

- Someone who believes "I must always be strong" may suppress feelings of sadness or vulnerability, creating a shadow that manifests as emotional numbness or difficulty forming close relationships.

- A person raised to believe "Money is the root of all evil" might repress their ambition, leading to inner conflict and self-sabotage in their career.

Exploring belief systems through shadow work helps us identify these hidden patterns and bring them into consciousness. Once we see how our beliefs have shaped our shadow, we can begin the process of integration and healing.

Identifying and Challenging Limiting Beliefs

Shadow work invites us to examine our beliefs with curiosity and honesty, asking whether they truly reflect our authentic self or if they have been inherited from family, culture, or society. This process begins with awareness:

1- Reflect on Your Beliefs: Take time to think about the ideas you hold about yourself and the world. Consider prompts such as:

- "What do I believe about my worthiness?"

- "What beliefs do I have about success, failure, or relationships?"

- "What emotions or traits have I suppressed because of these beliefs?"

2- Explore Their Origins: Once you identify a belief, ask where it came from. Did it originate from family, culture, religion, or personal experience? Recognizing the source helps separate your authentic self from inherited ideas.

3- Challenge Limiting Beliefs: Question the validity of beliefs that feel restrictive or unhelpful. For example:

- **Limiting Belief:** "I must always put others first."

- **Reframing:** "Caring for myself allows me to better care for others."

3- Replace with Empowering Beliefs: Create new beliefs that align with your values and goals. For instance:

- **Empowering Belief:** "I am worthy of love and acceptance, just as I am."

Aligning Beliefs with Your Authentic Self

Belief systems are not fixed. They are flexible and can evolve as you grow. Shadow work helps you uncover and challenge beliefs that no longer align with your authentic self, empowering you to replace them with ones that reflect your true values. This process creates space for healing, growth, and self-compassion, allowing you to live in alignment with your highest potential.

By understanding the role of beliefs in shaping the shadow, we take an essential step toward self- integration. Whether through journaling, tarot readings, or quiet reflection, exploring and transforming beliefs is a profound act of self-discovery—one that connects us to our inner truth and the divine wisdom that guides our journey.

Chapter 17

Imagination and Visualization

– Unlocking the Subconscious

Shadow work often requires us to dive into the hidden layers of our psyche, where words and logic sometimes fail to reach. Imagination and visualization offer a creative and powerful way to access the subconscious mind, where the shadow resides. By engaging with symbols, archetypes, and imagery, we can gently explore the suppressed parts of ourselves, integrate their lessons, and foster healing.

This chapter delves into the role of imagination and visualization in shadow work, offering practical techniques and showing how these tools can be combined with the Biblical Tarot: Shadows of the Soul to deepen self-awareness and transformation.

The Power of Imagination and Visualization in Shadow Work

Imagination is not merely a tool for creativity; it is a bridge to the subconscious mind. Visualization, as an extension of imagination, allows us to create mental scenarios, images, or narratives that bring hidden emotions, traits, and memories to the surface. These methods work because the subconscious communicates through symbols and metaphors, rather than words or logic.

By engaging in visualization exercises, we bypass the conscious mind's defenses—its tendency to deny, rationalize, or suppress—and provide the subconscious with a safe space to express itself. This opens the door to deeper self-understanding and healing.

Why Use Imagination and Visualization in Shadow Work?

Accessing the Subconscious:

The subconscious mind holds the shadow, making it inaccessible through direct reasoning. Visualization creates a non-threatening way to access these hidden parts, allowing them to reveal themselves through imagery or metaphors.

Creating a Safe Space:

Shadow work can bring up intense emotions, but visualization allows you to explore these feelings in a controlled and safe environment. For example, imagining a sacred space where you meet your shadow provides a mental container for exploration.

Engaging with Symbols and Archetypes:

The subconscious communicates in symbols, and archetypes often appear during shadow work. Visualization helps bring these symbols to life, allowing you to interact with them in meaningful ways.

Reframing and Healing:

Through imagination, you can revisit and reframe past experiences. Visualizing yourself responding differently to a painful memory can create new, empowering patterns that replace old, limiting ones.

Practical Visualization Exercises for Shadow Work

Here are a few exercises that combine imagination and shadow work:

1- Meeting Your Shadow:

- Close your eyes and imagine a safe, sacred space—a forest, a garden, or a cozy room. Picture yourself standing in this space, feeling grounded and calm.

- Invite your shadow to appear. It might take the form of a person, animal, or abstract energy. Allow it to communicate with you in any way it chooses, whether through words, images, or feelings.

  Ask questions like:

  » "What part of me do you represent?"

  » "What are you here to teach me?"

  » "How can I integrate you into my life?"

- When the interaction feels complete, thank your shadow for its guidance and gently return to your present state.

2- Inner Child Healing:

- Visualize yourself meeting your Inner Child in a nurturing, safe environment. Picture the child expressing their feelings—sadness, anger, fear, or joy.

- Offer comfort and validation to this part of yourself. You might visualize giving them a hug, a symbolic gift, or a word of reassurance, such as, "You are loved and safe."

- Reflect on how this exercise makes you feel and what it reveals about your current emotional needs.

3- Symbolic Journeys:

- Imagine embarking on a journey through a symbolic landscape, such as a cave, mountain, or river. Along the way, you might encounter figures, animals, or objects that represent aspects of your shadow.

- Reflect on the meaning of these symbols. For example, a locked door might symbolize a part of yourself you've been avoiding, while a bird might represent freedom or hope.

4- Revisiting Past Experiences:

- Choose a memory that evokes strong emotions, such as shame, fear, or regret. Visualize yourself stepping into the scene as you are now, offering comfort and guidance to your past self.

- Reframe the memory by imagining a different outcome, such as standing up for yourself or receiving the understanding you needed. This process helps release lingering pain and create a sense of resolution.

Visualization and the Biblical Tarot

The Biblical Tarot is an ideal tool for combining visualization with shadow work. Each card is rich with archetypal imagery, offering a gateway to the subconscious. Here are some ways to use the deck for imaginative exploration:

1- Stepping into the Cards:

- Select a card, such as The Shadow (Jacob Wrestles with God) or The Moon. Close your eyes and visualize yourself stepping into the scene depicted on the card.

- Imagine interacting with the elements of the card. For example, if you choose The Shadow, you might visualize yourself wrestling with a figure that represents your fears or limitations. Reflect on what the interaction reveals.

2- Creating a Narrative with a Spread:

- Lay out a three-card spread. Visualize yourself as the central figure moving through the narrative of the cards.

- For instance, imagine freeing yourself from the chains of The Devil, finding hope in The Star, and achieving wholeness in The World. Reflect on how this journey relates to your current challenges.

3- Meeting Archetypes:

- **Use visualization to meet the archetypes represented by the cards. For example:**

    » Visualize sitting with The High Priestess in a sacred temple, asking for guidance on an unresolved question.

Benefits of Visualization in Shadow Work

Here are some benefits of using visualization in your Shadow Work practice:

- **Deep Emotional Healing:**
  Visualization allows you to process emotions in a safe, symbolic way, reducing the risk of feeling overwhelmed or re-traumatized.

- **Enhanced Self-Awareness:**
  Imaginative exercises often reveal hidden truths about your desires, fears, and beliefs, providing deeper insights than rational analysis alone.

- **Creative Empowerment:**
  Visualization empowers you to rewrite old narratives, creating new, empowering patterns for the future.

- **Integration and Wholeness:**
  By interacting with shadow aspects through imagery, you create opportunities for acceptance and integration, fostering a sense of inner unity.

Practical Tips for Using Visualization

- **Set the Scene:**
  Choose a quiet, comfortable space where you won't be disturbed. Light a candle, play calming music, or use other rituals to signal that you're entering sacred inner work.

- **Stay Grounded:**
  Begin and end each session with grounding exercises, such as deep breathing, focusing on your physical sensa-

tions, or visualizing roots connecting you to the earth.

- **Trust the Process:**
  Let go of expectations and allow your imagination to unfold naturally. Whatever images or messages arise, trust that they hold meaning for your journey.

- **Journal Your Insights:**
  After each visualization, write down what you experienced. Reflect on the symbols, emotions, and lessons that emerged, and consider how they relate to your current shadow work.

Conclusion

Imagination and visualization are powerful allies in shadow work, connecting us to the subconscious and revealing hidden parts of ourselves. Through symbolic imagery, revisiting the past, and exploring archetypes, we unlock opportunities for healing and growth. Paired with the Biblical Tarot: Shadows of the Soul, these practices deepen self-awareness and guide us toward wholeness. Even the darkest shadows, when explored with imagination, hold the seeds of transformation and light.

Chapter 18

Alchemy and the Transformation of the Soul

In the ancient practice of alchemy, the goal was not simply to transform base metals into gold but to achieve spiritual enlightenment by transmuting the inner self. Alchemy's secret teachings reveal a powerful path of transformation that mirrors our own journey of shadow work, the process of facing and integrating the parts of ourselves that we often hide from view. Just as the alchemist worked through stages of purification, illumination, and unity, so too does shadow work guide us through self-discovery, healing, and spiritual awakening. This chapter explores the connection between alchemy and shadow work, revealing how the path to self-transformation is, at its heart, a process of turning inner "base metals" into the "gold" of wisdom, compassion, and wholeness.

The Stages of Alchemical Transformation and Shadow Work

Alchemy is a process of transformation through stages, each one representing a crucial step in breaking down the old self and creating something new. In shadow work, these alchemical stages map onto the phases we experience as we uncover, heal, and integrate the hidden aspects of our soul:

- **Nigredo (Blackening):** This is the first, dark stage in alchemy, representing dissolution. In shadow work, this is the phase where we confront the hidden parts of ourselves, facing painful emotions, suppressed memories, or unresolved conflicts. Like the alchemist, we dissolve outdated beliefs and behaviors, clearing the way for new growth.

- **Albedo (Whitening):** After breaking down the old, the alchemist purifies in the phase known as Albedo. For us, this is a time of self-compassion and clarity, where we begin to see ourselves more truthfully and accept our imperfections. Just as impurities are removed in alchemy, we release self-criticism, allowing compassion to fill the spaces where guilt and shame once lived.

- **Citrinitas (Yellowing):** Alchemists viewed Citrinitas as the stage of illumination, when insights emerge. In shadow work, this is where our understanding deepens, and we start seeing the wisdom in our shadows. We gain perspective, realizing that each shadow holds a lesson. Our new insights illuminate a way forward, guiding us to apply what we've learned to our lives.

- **Rubedo (Reddening):** The final stage of alchemy, Rubedo, represents union and the creation of the Philosopher's Stone. In shadow work, this is the phase of integration, where we unify all parts of ourselves, transforming pain into power, darkness into light. With this new wholeness, we achieve an inner peace and strength that aligns us with our higher self.

These stages emphasize that transformation is a process, and true growth often requires us to move through dark, uncomfortable places before we can emerge into the light.

From "Base Metals" to "Gold": Transforming Our Inner Selves

Alchemy's ultimate goal was to transform base metals into gold—a metaphor for inner transformation. Just as alchemists worked to refine metals, shadow work refines our inner lives. We enter the process burdened with "base" qualities: fear, resentment, anger, and self-doubt. By facing these aspects with courage and honesty, we transform them into the "gold" of wisdom, resilience, and compassion.

Shadow work challenges us to see that our fears, insecurities, and limitations are not weaknesses but rather untapped potential waiting to be transformed. By bringing these hidden aspects to light, we elevate them, turning our emotional and psychological burdens into strengths. Much like the alchemist's practice, this transformation takes time and commitment, yet the reward is a life that radiates inner wisdom and harmony.

The Philosopher's Stone: The Goal of Wholeness

The Philosopher's Stone was believed to grant the alchemist both enlightenment and eternal life. In the context of shadow work, the Philosopher's Stone symbolizes the achievement of self- integration and wholeness. As we progress through shadow work, we begin to reconcile our light and shadow aspects, creating a unified self. This journey requires acceptance of all aspects of who we are—our hopes, dreams, fears, and flaws. Only by integrating these parts can we experience true peace and balance.

The Philosopher's Stone is also a reminder that enlightenment is not found by rejecting our humanity but by embracing it fully. It is the understanding that our divine potential lies within the very aspects of ourselves we sometimes wish to hide. Through shadow work, we don't discard our shadows; instead, we learn to appreciate them as integral pieces of our whole self.

Solve et Coagula: Dissolve and Reunite

In alchemy, the principle of Solve et Coagula—"dissolve and reunite"—describes the continuous process of breaking down the old self and rebuilding a more integrated, evolved self. In shadow work, this principle becomes a guiding philosophy.

- **Solve (Dissolve):** Here, we let go of rigid beliefs, attachments, and habits that no longer serve us. This is the act of dissolving our illusions and outdated patterns.

- **Coagula (Reunite):** After breaking down the old, we rebuild our lives, this time with greater awareness and a renewed sense of purpose.

Shadow work is a continuous cycle of letting go and reforming, each time bringing us closer to a deeper understanding of ourselves. By engaging with this process, we repeatedly refine and elevate ourselves, just as the alchemist refines substances in search of gold.

The Alchemist's Journey as the Journey of Self

Alchemy is as much a journey of the soul as it is a scientific process. The alchemist, much like the practitioner of shadow work, undergoes their own transformation, learning and evolving at every stage. This inner journey requires curiosity, humility, and resilience, as each phase challenges the alchemist to let go of false ideas and embrace growth.

For those on the path of shadow work, the journey mirrors that of the alchemist. It involves facing difficult truths, experimenting with new ways of being, and evolving through trial and error. Shadow work asks us to be both the "alchemist" and the "lead"—to apply our wisdom to ourselves, refining and transmuting our inner lives.

Balancing Opposites: The Path to Wholeness

Alchemy emphasizes the need to balance opposing forces—light and dark, masculine and feminine, spirit and matter. This balance reflects the goal of shadow work, which is to integrate our conscious and unconscious aspects. Rather than denying or suppressing our shadow, we learn to acknowledge and accept it. This creates a balanced, grounded self capable of moving between light and shadow with grace and wisdom.

As in alchemy, personal growth is not about achieving a "pure" or "perfect" self but rather a whole self. The work is in harmonizing our strengths and vulnerabilities, learning to live fully and authentically by embracing all aspects of who we are.

Discovering the "Inner Gold" or Divine Self

In alchemy, "inner gold" is a metaphor for spiritual awakening and enlightenment. Shadow work is, in essence, the pursuit of this inner gold. By working through our darker aspects and hidden fears, we uncover valuable qualities such as resilience, insight, and a higher sense of purpose.

This inner gold, or divine self, represents the part of us that has been purified through the trials of shadow work. It is the self that has grown stronger through adversity, more compassionate through understanding, and more wise through experience.

The journey to the inner gold is not an easy one, but it is deeply rewarding. Each time we confront a shadow, we gain a new layer of wisdom; each time we integrate a hidden part of ourselves, we experience greater harmony. The inner gold is the light within that we reveal by moving through the darkness. This inner transformation becomes a source of guidance, helping us live in alignment with our true purpose.

Alchemy and Shadow Work: A Path of Transformation

Alchemy teaches us that transformation is a journey of cycles, each stage building on the last. In shadow work, we are alchemists of the soul, refining ourselves through awareness, acceptance, and integration. By dissolving our illusions and embracing all aspects of ourselves, we reach a place of inner wholeness.

This journey of turning base metals into gold is ultimately a journey of love and self-acceptance. Through shadow work, we learn that our true power lies not in denying our shadows but in transforming them. This transformation brings us closer to our divine nature, creating a life that reflects the beauty, strength, and wisdom we have uncovered within. Just as alchemists sought to create gold, we, too, discover that our highest potential shines brightest when we have fully embraced both our light and our shadow.

Chapter 19

Archetypes in Tarot and the Process of Shadow Work

"The Kingdom of God is within you." – Luke 17:21
(An invitation to remember that the vast landscape of our inner world,
with all its light and shadow, is a sacred place.)

Archetypes are like hidden rivers running through our minds—silent yet mighty, shaping our perceptions and directing the flow of our lives beneath the surface of our awareness. In the Tarot, we find these archetypes depicted on every card: from the innocent, wandering Fool to the regal Emperor, these symbols echo eternal human experiences.

For those working with the Biblical Tarot: Shadows of the Soul, each card embodies a character or story drawn from Scripture, and in these narratives, we discover deep-rooted patterns that have guided humanity for millennia. Biblical tales naturally stir strong emotions—reverence, curiosity, even discomfort—and these reactions offer profound clues about which parts of our psyche need tending, healing, or celebrating. This is precisely why Tarot, particularly when interwoven with Scripture, can serve as such a catalyst for shadow work: it brings the hidden corners of our being into the light, helping us transform what once was buried into a source of wisdom.

Archetypes and Jungian Psychology

Swiss psychiatrist Carl Jung introduced the concept of the collective unconscious, a vast psychic heritage that transcends individual experience. Within this collective realm dwell the archetypes—universal images and motifs such as the Hero, the Mother, the Wise Man, and the Trickster. These elemental forces are found in myths, fairy tales, and religious traditions around the globe, suggesting that, despite our diverse cultures, we share a shared bedrock of symbolic language.

Universal vs. Personal Archetypes

Though archetypes are universal, they manifest uniquely in each individual's life. Think of them like a set of musical notes that can be arranged in infinite compositions. A single biblical story, such as Moses leading the Israelites out of Egypt, may speak to the universal longing for freedom and deliverance. On a personal level, however, you might relate to Moses's doubts or frustration—perhaps you've felt called to lead or teach despite your own insecurities. This layering of universal meaning with deeply personal resonance is what makes archetypes so powerful in self-reflection.

Archetypes as Timeless Symbols

Influence on Dreams, Culture, and Personal Growth

It's no accident that certain images and storylines recur in our dreams. Whether you dream of being pursued or of uncovering a hidden treasure, these motifs often represent an archetype speaking directly to your inner world. Culturally, archetypes are immortalized in literature, religion, and art. The stories of Adam and Eve, David and Goliath, or Ruth and Naomi all illuminate patterns of vulnerability, courage, devotion, and sacrifice. By recognizing these archetypal roots within ourselves, we gain insight into what lies beneath the surface of our consciousness.

From Greek myths to Eastern folklore, we see echoes of these biblical narratives. Creation myths, redemption arcs, and tales of moral testing often overlap in their core messages, pointing to a deep, shared human story. Through their triumphs and trials, biblical figures like Noah, Esther, and Job mirror archetypes we continually reenact—resilience in the face of calamity, faith amidst uncertainty, and transformation through suffering.

Archetypes and Decision-Making

Archetypes often work behind the scenes, influencing how we respond to challenges. You might take on the "hero" role in conflicts, stepping forward to protect or defend, or, conversely, find yourself stuck in a "victim" mindset, feeling that life happens to you rather than through you. By identifying which archetype (or combination of archetypes) is stirring within at pivotal moments, you can transform reactive choices into conscious ones.

Self-Growth Through Archetypal Awareness

When you become aware of an archetype at play, you learn to channel it in healthier, more authentic ways. For instance, the "king/queen" archetype might manifest as authoritarian control or benevolent leadership. By recognizing its presence, you can temper your approach, guiding others with compassion rather than dominating them from insecurity. Awareness is the first step towards mastery.

Integrating Archetypal Knowledge in Self-Analysis

Practical Techniques

- **Journaling:** Keep a record of recurring symbols in your dreams or daily life. Write down any biblical stories or verses that resonate strongly, or any images from the Biblical Tarot that keep surfacing in your mind.

- **Mindful Observation:** Notice when you feel drawn to certain characters or repelled by others—both in Scripture and in your real-life interactions. Ask yourself which archetype might be pressing for recognition.

- **Self-Inquiry:** Pose questions like, "Am I acting out the Victim, the Warrior, or the Sage?" "Which biblical story feels closest to my current life situation?"

The Biblical Tarot: Shadows of the Soul offers a vivid lens for this work. Each card is a mirror of a scriptural event or figure, revealing where an archetype may be influencing you from the shadows. By discerning your emotional reactions to a card, you gain a clearer view of the deeper patterns shaping your behavior.

Shadow Work with the Biblical Tarot: Shadows of the Soul

The "shadow" is that portion of ourselves which we deem unacceptable—feelings we hide, traits we deny, or parts of our personal story we keep in the dark. Jung saw this as the reservoir of unacknowledged, often powerful energies that continue to influence us, even though we might not be conscious of them. Shadow work is the process of recognizing, understanding, and embracing these hidden aspects so that they no longer wield destructive power.

Utilizing Archetypes for Shadow Integration

- **Draw a Card:** Whether you are seeking guidance on a specific issue or just exploring your psyche, select a card from the Biblical Tarot deck.

- **Identify the Biblical Archetype:** Reflect on the story depicted—who are the key figures? What central theme stands out (e.g., betrayal, redemption, sacrifice)?

- **Notice Emotional Reactions:** Pay special attention to discomfort. Do you feel judgmental, disturbed, or oddly fascinated by the imagery? These emotional currents often signal an unexamined aspect of your shadow.

- **Ask Guiding Questions:** "How might I be embodying this biblical archetype in my life?" or "What about this story do I resist, and why?"

- **Journal and Meditate:** Write down your insights, letting the biblical narrative illuminate your own inner conflicts or aspirations. In meditation, visualize the card's imagery and invite its lessons to unfold.

Examples of Shadow Integration

•   Adam and Eve (The Lovers): Beyond the romantic aspect, this story highlights choice, temptation, and personal accountability. Shadow work may reveal where we resist owning our decisions or where shame and guilt keep us stuck.

•   The Tower of Babel (The Tower): Symbolizing ambition and pride, the Tower's fall can point to our fear of losing control or status. By examining where we crave power or fear vulnerability, we begin to soften pride into humility, transforming chaos into growth.

The Major Arcana
as a Five-Stage Spiritual Journey

When viewed as a continuous narrative, the Major Arcana reveals a universal path toward greater self-awareness and spiritual maturity. Just as biblical stories guide us through themes of faith, struggle, redemption, and transformation, the tarot's archetypal figures trace a similar unfolding in our personal lives. In this framework, each cluster of Major Arcana cards represents a distinct phase of the journey, reminding us that every quest for wholeness must pass through cycles of challenge, renewal, and illumination.

1. **Beginning of Self-Discovery – Identity, Relationships, Faith**
   This first phase mirrors the moment we hear an inner call—much like Abraham stepping into the unknown or Adam and Eve tasting the fruit of self-awareness. We discover our identity, test our faith, and forge relationships that shape our worldview. Cards like The Soul, The Magician, The High Priestess, The Empress, The Emperor, and The High Priest depict the foundational figures and lessons that initiate the pilgrim's path. Here, we learn the importance of curiosity, the power of creation, the depth of intuition, and the role of guidance—both paternal and maternal, physical and spiritual.

2. **Confronting Challenges and External Tests**
   Once our sense of self is formed, real-world trials inevitably arrive. Like the Israelites venturing through the desert, or David facing Goliath, we must grapple with forces that test our resolve. Cards such as The Chariot, Strength, The Hermit, and The Wheel of Life represent the practical challenges of human life, teaching discipline, resilience, and faith in divine timing. In wrestling with external obstacles, we learn not to succumb to fear or complacency but to meet life's tests with courage and devotion.

3. **Deep Inner Work and Transformation**
   In the third stage, our struggles turn inward. We realize the greatest battles are often fought within our own hearts and

minds. Cards like Justice, The Hanged Man, Death, and Temperance symbolize the call to examine our morality, to let go of familiar but limiting perspectives, and to embrace profound change. This is the crucible of transformation—where sacrifice, forgiveness, and authentic realignment must occur before growth can continue. Biblically, this resonates with Jonah's solitary time in the belly of the whale or Jesus's willingness to surrender in Gethsemane.

4. **The Dark Night of the Soul**
   After glimpsing our inner depths, we encounter the densest shadows. This phase can feel like spiritual desolation—yet it is here that illusions shatter and hidden truths emerge. The Devil, The Tower, The Star, and The Moon illustrate the intensity of confronting our own darkness, the collapse of false structures, and the fragile yet unwavering hope that lights our way forward. Stories like the Tower of Babel or the Garden of Gethsemane highlight humanity's tendency to wrestle with pride, temptation, and fear—lessons that ultimately guide us toward humility, redemption, and renewed vision.

5. **Illumination, Awakening, and Completion**
   Having traversed both light and shadow, the final stage brings a profound realization of unity and grace. The last cards—The Sun, Judgement, and The World—announce the dawning of clear sight, spiritual rebirth, and the joy of wholeness. This echoes the scriptural promises of resurrection, redemption, and the revelation of a new heaven and earth. Yet the journey does not end here—like the endless cycles of life, every completion births a new beginning, inviting us to keep growing in wisdom, compassion, and faith.

Together, these five stages show the Major Arcana as more than just 22 separate images—it is a single blend reflecting the timeless dance between struggle and surrender, darkness and light, ego and the divine. By recognizing where we stand within this arc, we can navigate our own inner pilgrimage with deeper awareness and reverence, knowing that at each twist and turn of the path, we are guided by archetypal forces that have shaped the human spirit for millennia.

Card	Archetype
0. The Soul	The Innocent / The Pilgrim / The Child

Theme: Innocent faith, stepping into the unknown with trust.

Shadow Work Tip: Notice where reckless behavior or naïveté might sabotage you. Are you jumping in without discernment, or avoiding growth due to fear?

Journal Prompt: "Where in my life am I being nudged to take a leap of faith? What fears or doubts arise when I consider stepping forward?"

Card	Archetype
1. The Magician	The Manifestor / The Alchemist / Sorcerer

Theme: Harnessing divine power, turning vision into reality.

Shadow Work Tip: Observe if you're over-manipulating situations or underestimating your abilities. Where do you feel powerless, and how can you reclaim agency?

Journal Prompt: "How do I use my talents and resources? Do I channel them for a higher purpose, or do I misdirect them out of fear or ego?"

Card	Archetype
2. The High Priestess	The Mystic / The Seer / Anima

Theme: Intuitive knowledge, sacred insight, hidden wisdom.

Shadow Work Tip: Examine your resistance to inner knowing. Do you dismiss your intuition, or hide aspects of yourself out of fear of judgment?

Journal Prompt: "What truths lie beneath my daily awareness? What message is my intuition trying to convey right now?"

Card	Archetype
3. The Empress	The Nurturer / The Mother

Theme: Nurturing, abundance, the creative and life-giving force.

Shadow Work Tip: Check for codependency or neglect of self-care. Are you giving too much and depleting yourself, or withholding nurturing from yourself or others?

Journal Prompt: "In what ways can I cultivate greater self-love and nurture those around me without losing my own balance?"

The Major Arcana as a Spiritual Journey – Stage 1 (Cards 0–6)

BEGINNING OF SELF-DISCOVERY – IDENTITY, RELATIONSHIPS, FAITH

Card	Archetype
4. The Emperor	The Ruler / The Patriarch / The Father

Theme: Authority, stability, fatherly leadership.

Shadow Work Tip: Reflect on your relationship with control. Do you become rigid, or do you avoid responsibility?

Journal Prompt: "What parts of my life need better boundaries and leadership? How can I establish structure in a compassionate way?"

Card	Archetype
5. The High Priest	The Teacher / Spiritual Guide / Sage

Theme: Tradition, religious guidance, collective belief systems.

Shadow Work Tip: Observe whether you're blindly following rules or rebelling against them. Where have you internalized dogma without question?

Journal Prompt: "What teachings have shaped my worldview? Which do I embrace authentically, and which ones no longer serve me?"

Card	Archetype
6. The Lovers	The Union / Choice / Lovers / Anima-Animus

Theme: Love, relationships, pivotal choices that shape our path.

Shadow Work Tip: Notice where fear of intimacy or fear of being alone drives your decisions. Are you making choices that honor both yourself and the other?

Journal Prompt: "What important choice am I facing? How can I align my head and heart to ensure it is made in integrity and love?"

The Major Arcana as a Spiritual Journey – Stage 1 (Cards 0–6)

BEGINNING OF SELF-DISCOVERY – IDENTITY, RELATIONSHIPS, FAITH

Card	Archetype
7. The Chariot	The Warrior / Determination

Theme: Determination, willpower, triumph through discipline.

Shadow Work Tip: Look at areas of your life where you might be bulldozing over others—or avoiding challenges altogether.

Journal Prompt: "Where am I being called to assert my willpower? How can I balance ambition with compassion?"

8. Strength	The Hero / Courageous / Inner Fortitude

Theme: Inner fortitude, courage, channeling passion constructively.

Shadow Work Tip: Notice if you force control through aggression or if you shy away from challenges out of fear. How can you meet difficulties with gentle strength?

Journal Prompt: "What situation in my life is testing my inner fortitude, and how can I respond with both strength and compassion?"

9. The Hermit	The Wise One / Solitary Seeker

Theme: Solitude, introspection, spiritual retreat.

Shadow Work Tip: Examine any fears of loneliness or resistance to solitude. Are you hiding from the world or avoiding necessary reflection?

Journal Prompt: "How can I carve out time for quiet introspection? What truths emerge when I allow silence in my life?"

10. The Wheel of Life	The Cycle / Divine Timing / Fate

Theme: Cycles of destiny, divine timing, life's unforeseen turns.

Shadow Work Tip: Acknowledge where you feel stuck, helpless, or overly controlling about outcomes. How do you respond to change?

Journal Prompt: "What cycle or season am I in right now? Where can I practice acceptance and flow with life's shifts?"

Card	Archetype
11. Justice	The Judge / Equilibrium

Theme: Balance, fairness, moral discernment, consequences.

Shadow Work Tip: Look for where you might be judging yourself or others too harshly. Are you unwilling to accept responsibility for your actions?

Journal Prompt: "Where in my life am I being called to restore balance or make amends? How can I exercise compassion in my decisions?"

12. The Hanged Man	The Martyr / The Surrender / Sacrifice

Theme: Surrender, new perspective, suspension.

Shadow Work Tip: Reflect on resistance to relinquishing control. Is pride or fear preventing you from seeing a situation differently?

Journal Prompt: "Where am I being called to surrender my ego or old beliefs? What fresh insight might I gain from doing so?"

13. Death	The Transformer / Endings & Beginnings

Theme: Endings, metamorphosis, shedding old identities.

Shadow Work Tip: Identify what you're clinging to that no longer serves your growth. Are you resisting necessary endings out of fear of change?

Journal Prompt: "What aspect of my life or identity is ready to be shed? How might letting it go open space for a new beginning?"

14. Temperance	The Healer / Balance / Harmony

Theme: Moderation, harmonizing opposites, spiritual alchemy.

Shadow Work Tip: Look for extremes in your behavior—overindulgence or rigid austerity. Where can you bring in gentle moderation?

Journal Prompt: "How can I cultivate more balance in my life? Which areas need alchemy and integration rather than all-or-nothing thinking?"

The Major Arcana as a Spiritual Journey – Stage 3 (Cards 11–14)
DEEP INNER WORK AND TRANSFORMATION

Card	Archetype
15. The Devil	The Tempter / Shadow Self

Theme: Temptation, bondage, illusions, confronting the darker self.

Shadow Work Tip: Identify obsessions, addictions, or negative thought loops. Where can you bring compassion to the parts of you that feel trapped?

Journal Prompt: "What do I feel enslaved by—habits, fears, relationships? How can I gently reclaim my freedom and self-worth?"

Card	Archetype
16. The Tower	The Destroyer / The Trickster / Collapse / Reckoning

Theme: Sudden upheaval, destruction of false constructs, revelation.

Shadow Work Tip: Consider what structures or illusions you've built that may be unhealthy. Are you ignoring signs that a shake-up is needed?

Journal Prompt: "Where in my life is pride or stubbornness blocking growth? How can I rebuild with greater integrity once the old falls away?"

Card	Archetype
17. The Star	The Visionary / The Beacon / Hope

Theme: Hope, divine guidance, renewal after chaos.

Shadow Work Tip: When despair or cynicism sets in, reflect on hope. Have you lost faith in yourself or in a higher guidance?

Journal Prompt: "What inspires hope in me right now, despite challenges? Where can I look for signs of renewal in my life?"

Card	Archetype
18. The Moon	The Dreamer / Illusion / The Psyche (Anima-Animus interplay)

Theme: Mystery, illusion, subconscious stirrings, emotional testing.

Shadow Work Tip: Pay attention to anxieties or illusions that keep you stuck. Is there a pattern of self-deception or avoidance of deeper truths?

Journal Prompt: "What recurring dreams or anxieties might be trying to reveal about my inner world? How can I gently bring them into conscious light?"

The Major Arcana as a Spiritual Journey - STAGE 4 (Cards 15–18)
THE DARK NIGHT OF THE SOUL

Card	Archetype
19. The Sun	The Enlightened Child / The Illuminator / Clarity
Theme: Joy, enlightenment, clarity, rebirth into the light.	
Shadow Work Tip: Even positivity can cast a shadow if it denies real pain. Notice whether "false cheer" covers up deeper issues.	
Journal Prompt: "What truths, once fully embraced, would bring me the greatest sense of freedom and joy? How can I share my light without denying my shadows?"	
20. Judgement	The Redeemer / The Awakening / Rebirth
Theme: Awakening, accountability, rebirth at a higher vibration.	
Shadow Work Tip: Examine self-criticism or fear of being 'found unworthy.' How can releasing shame or guilt help you hear your true calling?	
Journal Prompt: "In what ways am I being called to 'awaken' or answer a deeper purpose? What judgment or limiting belief stands in my way?"	
21. The World	The Self (Individuation) / The Wholeness / Completion
Theme: Wholeness, cosmic unity, completion of one journey and the start of another.	
Shadow Work Tip: Sometimes completion triggers fear of the unknown next step. Are you hesitating to celebrate your achievements or move into a new chapter?	
Journal Prompt: "What major cycle in my life is reaching completion? How can I honor this ending and embrace the new horizon opening before me?"	

The Major Arcana as a Spiritual Journey – Stage 5 (Cards 19–21)
ILLUMINATION, AWAKENING, AND COMPLETION

Part II

Walking the Path:

A Guide to
The Biblical Tarot

Chapter 20

Understanding the Biblical Tarot: Shadows of the Soul

The Biblical Tarot: Shadows of the Soul is a unique tarot deck designed to guide users through the transformative process of shadow work—the exploration and integration of the hidden, often challenging parts of ourselves. This deck offers a path to confront deep-seated emotions, unresolved conflicts, and hidden fears, helping us understand and integrate these "shadows" in a way that fosters healing and personal growth. With its foundation in biblical narratives and wisdom, this deck not only serves as a tool for self-reflection but also as a spiritual guide, rooted in timeless teachings.

Purpose of the Deck

The purpose of the Biblical Tarot: Shadows of the Soul is to shine light on the parts of ourselves we often avoid—our fears, insecurities, and suppressed feelings. Many of us carry these hidden aspects in our subconscious, where they influence our behavior, often without our awareness.

This deck addresses that by allowing us to uncover these hidden emotions and face them with clarity, compassion, and a deeper understanding rooted in spiritual and biblical insights.

This deck stands out because it combines traditional tarot wisdom with biblical stories and symbols. Each card is inspired by a biblical narrative or character, offering insight into both light and shadow aspects. By connecting with these stories, users find not only psychological insights but also moral and spiritual guidance. The deck uniquely blends shadow work with biblical teachings, allowing seekers to work through their shadows with a grounded sense of purpose, faith, and divine connection.

Structure of the Deck

The Biblical Tarot: Shadows of the Soul is structured similarly to a traditional tarot deck, divided into the Major Arcana and Minor Arcana. Each section serves a different purpose, guiding the user through both profound spiritual lessons and the everyday experiences that shape our lives.

The Major Arcana:
Key Life Lessons and Spiritual Growth

The Major Arcana consists of 22 cards, each representing significant stages in our spiritual journey and life lessons. In the context of shadow work, these cards highlight the larger, often karmic themes that shape our lives and challenge us to grow. Each card in the Major Arcana tells a story inspired by a biblical figure or event, depicting a particular phase in the journey of the soul—from innocence to wisdom, from challenge to transformation.

When a Major Arcana card appears in a reading, it signifies an important milestone in personal growth, pointing to a life lesson, a divine intervention, or a major challenge that requires our attention. These cards are associated with pivotal moments that urge us to face our shadows and evolve toward our full potential. In the Shadows of the Soul edition, the Major Arcana becomes a spiritual guide, highlighting opportunities for enlightenment, redemption, and deeper connection to one's faith and higher self.

The Minor Arcana:
The Four Suits and Daily Guidance

The Minor Arcana consists of 56 cards and is divided into four suits: Candles, Chalices, Feathers, and Grains. While the Major Arcana provides a broad spiritual overview, the Minor Arcana delves into the practical, day-to-day elements of our lives, focusing on our thoughts, emotions, actions, and material well-being. Each suit represents an element and a different aspect of the human experience, offering insight into the smaller yet significant moments that impact our personal growth.

- **Candles (Fire Element):** The suit of Candles represents the drive for growth, ambition, creativity, and inspiration. Linked to the element of Fire, it symbolizes energy, motivation, and the spark that ignites change. Cards in the Candles suit shed light on our inner passions, the forces that drive us forward, and the shadows of pride, impatience, or burnout that can arise when our inner fire is out of balance.

- **Chalices (Water Element):** The suit of Chalices reflects the realm of emotions, relationships, intuition, and creativity. Associated with the element of Water, this suit delves into the fluidity of our inner lives, including how we connect with others and our emotional needs. Chalices encourage us to embrace love, empathy, and compassion while helping us confront emotional wounds, fears of vulnerability, and suppressed feelings.

- **Feathers (Air Element):** The suit of Feathers is tied to thought, intellect, communication, and action. Representing the element of Air, Feathers explore the realm of the mind, focusing on logic, perception, and expression. This suit invites us to examine our beliefs, thought patterns, and communication skills, as well as to confront mental shadows like self-doubt, criticism, or anxiety.

- **Grains (Earth Element):** The suit of Grains represents the material aspects of life, including our physical world, career, finances, and health. Connected to the element of Earth, Grains remind us to stay grounded, practical, and mindful of our resources. Cards in this suit help us understand our relationship with security, abundance, and stability while encouraging us to confront fears of scarcity, insecurity, or over-attachment to material success.

Each suit in the Minor Arcana offers a window into a different part of ourselves. By examining these cards, we gain insight into our thoughts, emotions, motivations, and material concerns.

Together, the suits reveal the complex interplay of these elements in our lives and how each aspect contributes to our personal growth or holds us back when out of balance.

A Journey Through the Shadows and Toward the Soul

The Biblical Tarot: Shadows of the Soul serves as a map for those seeking to understand and integrate the shadow parts of their personality. By working with both the Major and Minor Arcana, users are guided through the significant stages of spiritual growth and the everyday choices that shape their journey. This deck is a reminder that every experience—whether a grand spiritual revelation or a small emotional struggle—carries within it the potential for transformation.

The unique structure of the Biblical Tarot offers a profound experience of self-discovery, helping individuals face their shadows, elevate their emotional frequency, and walk a path toward healing and inner peace. Through this sacred journey, each card becomes a step closer to integrating all parts of oneself, moving from darkness into light, from shadow into soul.

Chapter 21

The Shadow Card

The Story of Jacob Wrestling with God

In the Biblical Tarot: Shadows of the Soul, the Shadow card is a powerful representation of the inner struggle inherent in shadow work. It draws its meaning from the biblical story of Jacob wrestling with God, found in Genesis 32:22-32. This story marks a pivotal moment in Jacob's life—a time of transformation, confrontation, and, ultimately, redemption.

The story unfolds as Jacob, alone in the night, wrestles with a mysterious figure until dawn. This figure is revealed to be God, and through the struggle, Jacob's name is changed to Israel, symbolizing his new identity and a renewed relationship with God. Jacob's wrestling with God reflects the internal battle we all face when confronting the hidden, repressed parts of ourselves—the shadow.

This card reminds us that shadow work is not an easy process. It is a wrestling with the unknown, a struggle to reconcile the parts of ourselves that we've kept hidden. Just as Jacob fought through the night, shadow work requires us to face our fears, our past, and the unresolved emotions that have shaped our identity. But, like Jacob, through this process, we emerge transformed.

The Shadow Card in Shadow Work

The Shadow card represents the process of shadow work itself—a confrontation with the inner parts of our soul that have been neglected or repressed. This card appears when we are being called to delve deeper into our unconscious, to wrestle with the parts of ourselves that we find difficult to accept. It is both a challenge and an invitation to engage with the deepest parts of our psyche.

Key Meanings of the Shadow Card:

- **Confronting Inner Conflict:** Just as Jacob wrestled with God, this card represents the inner conflict between our conscious self and the shadow. It calls us to face the difficult truths about ourselves, including our fears, weaknesses, and unresolved emotions.

- **Transformation Through Struggle:** The Shadow card reminds us that transformation often comes through struggle. Just as Jacob was blessed and renamed after his encounter, we too can experience growth, healing, and a new sense of identity when we confront and integrate our shadows.

- **Facing the Unknown:** The night symbolizes the unknown and the unconscious. The Shadow card asks us to enter the darkness of our inner world, trusting that by engaging with what we find there, we will come into the light of new understanding.

- **A Call to Self-Awareness:** This card invites deep self-reflection. It asks the question: "What part of myself am I resisting?" By reflecting on this question, we begin the process of bringing our shadows into the light of conscious awareness, allowing for integration and healing.

The Meaning of the Moon Symbol

The Shadow card is marked by a crescent moon, a symbol rich with meaning. In many cultures and spiritual traditions, the moon is associated with the subconscious, intuition, and the cycles of life. The moon's phases reflect the cycles of growth, decay, and renewal that we experience in both our inner and outer worlds. The crescent moon, in particular, represents a moment of transition—a sliver of light breaking through the darkness, symbolizing hope, potential, and new beginnings.

Key Meanings of the Moon Symbol:

- **Emerging Light from Darkness:** The crescent moon on the Shadow card reflects the process of shadow work itself—a journey from darkness to light. As we wrestle with our inner shadows, we gradually bring them into the light of conscious awareness, allowing us to see the parts of ourselves that have been hidden.

- **Intuition and Inner Guidance:** The crescent moon is often associated with intuition, reminding us that the journey through shadow work requires not just intellectual understanding but a deep trust in our inner guidance. It encourages us to rely on our instincts and spiritual insight as we navigate the process.

- **Transformation and Cycles:** The crescent moon represents the early stages of growth and transformation. It symbolizes the potential for change that exists when we begin the process of shadow work. Just as the moon moves through phases, our shadow work follows a cyclical process of discovery, confrontation, and healing.

The crescent moon also reminds us that transformation is not immediate—it takes time, just as the moon slowly grows from crescent to full. This symbol encourages patience and trust in the process, knowing that with persistence, the light will eventually break through.

Interpreting the Shadow Card in Readings

When the Shadow card appears in a reading, it signals that the time has come to face a significant aspect of your shadow. It may be revealing an internal conflict you've been avoiding, a fear that's been holding you back, or a pattern of behavior that no longer serves you. This card calls for self-awareness and courage, asking you to look within and wrestle with the parts of yourself that are hidden in darkness.

Reflection Questions for the Shadow Card:
What internal struggle am I currently facing?

- What part of myself am I resisting or avoiding?

- How can I embrace this struggle as an opportunity for transformation?

- What fears or unresolved emotions are rising to the surface?

- What light can I find within this period of darkness?

The Shadow card often arrives during moments of significant transition or personal growth. It is a reminder that shadow work is not meant to be easy, but it is essential for healing and transformation. The card encourages you to trust the process and to have faith that, like Jacob, you will emerge from the struggle with a renewed sense of identity and purpose.

Using the Shadow Card in Your Shadow Work Practice

Incorporating the Shadow card into your shadow work practice can deepen your exploration of the subconscious and provide guidance for confronting your inner conflicts. Here are some ways to use the Shadow card as a tool for self-reflection:

- **Focused Meditation:**
  Place the Shadow card in front of you during meditation, focusing on the story of Jacob wrestling with God. As you meditate, reflect on your own inner struggles. What are you currently wrestling with in your life? Allow the card's energy to guide you toward deeper self-awareness.

- **Shadow Work Journaling:**
  Use the Shadow card as a prompt for journaling. Write about a part of yourself that you've been resisting or suppressing. How can you confront this shadow with courage and compassion? Let the story of Jacob inspire you to engage with your shadow work, trusting that transformation will come through the process.

- **Integration with Tarot Spreads:**
  Include the Shadow card in your tarot spreads when you're focusing on inner conflict or major personal transformations. The card can help clarify what part of your shadow needs attention and offer guidance on how to navigate the struggle with grace and self-compassion.

Conclusion:
Embracing the Struggle for Transformation

The Shadow card in the Biblical Tarot: Shadows of the Soul is a profound reminder that transformation comes through struggle. Like Jacob, we are called to wrestle with the parts of ourselves that have been hidden in darkness. This card teaches us that shadow work is not a one-time event but an ongoing process of self-discovery, healing, and renewal.

The crescent moon symbolizes the light that begins to emerge from the darkness, reminding us that through patience, reflection, and courage, we can bring our shadows into the light and experience true transformation. When the Shadow card appears, it is an invitation to embrace the struggle, knowing that through it, you will emerge stronger, wiser, and more aligned with your true self.

Chapter 22

Biblical Tarot as a Spiritual Companion for Transformation

The Biblical Tarot: Shadows of the Soul is much more than a traditional tarot deck; it is a spiritual companion on the path to self-discovery, healing, and growth. Designed to guide users through both light and shadow aspects of their soul, it offers a unique bridge between faith and self-reflection. This chapter explores how the Biblical Tarot serves as a trusted ally in the journey toward spiritual maturity, helping us confront our hidden shadows, embrace our divine potential, and move closer to the peace and wholeness we seek.

Embracing the Deck as a Spiritual Companion

The purpose of the Biblical Tarot: Shadows of the Soul is to walk alongside you on your journey, offering insights and guidance inspired by biblical teachings. Unlike traditional tarot decks that are often associated with fortune-telling, this deck is not about predicting the future. Instead, it's about understanding the self, uncovering truths, and experiencing healing by exploring both the divine and human aspects of our soul. The cards offer support, insight, and wisdom, just as a close companion would, providing a safe space to examine our inner world.

Each card invites us to pause and reflect, guiding us through the stories of biblical figures who faced their own shadows and overcame trials. As you explore this deck, you'll find that each card can become a mirror of your own spiritual journey, reflecting the areas where you're called to grow, heal, and release what no longer serves you. In this way, the deck becomes a gentle but transformative presence—a spiritual friend encouraging you to embrace self-knowledge and compassion, both for yourself and others.

Each Card as a Reflection of Light and Shadow

In the Biblical Tarot: Shadows of the Soul, each card represents both light and shadow aspects. Just as biblical figures like David, Moses, and Mary Magdalene had their strengths and flaws, so too does each card reveal the duality within us. The light side of each card offers insight into our divine qualities, our potential for love, kindness, and wisdom. The shadow side, however, confronts us with our fears, doubts, insecurities, and tendencies that hold us back from growth.

For example, the Soul card, which replaces the traditional Fool, symbolizes the journey of the soul in all its innocence and potential. In its light aspect, it represents openness to life, curiosity, and willingness to learn. In its shadow, however, it reflects naivety, ungrounded idealism, or avoidance of responsibility. By acknowledging both sides, we can use each card to explore the areas where we excel as well as those where we struggle.

This duality allows us to see both our strengths and limitations, helping us integrate all aspects of ourselves. The light side reminds us of our inherent goodness, while the shadow side highlights where growth is needed. Together, they provide a balanced view that fosters self-compassion and encourages us to work toward inner harmony.

Bridging Faith and Self-Reflection

For those who wish to explore their inner world without losing touch with their faith, Biblical Tarot: Shadows of the Soul serves as a bridge between spirituality and self-reflection. Shadow work, the process of examining the parts of ourselves we often hide, can be challenging, especially for those who may feel a conflict between their spiritual beliefs and traditional practices like tarot. This deck eases that tension by rooting the exploration of the shadow self in biblical stories and teachings, making the process accessible and meaningful for those with a Christian perspective.

Each card provides a story or figure from the Bible that mirrors the complexities of the human soul. For instance, Jacob wrestling with God represents the inner struggle we face when we confront our shadows. His journey serves as a powerful example of the faith and courage it takes to acknowledge and work through our hidden fears and insecurities. By connecting the shadow self with spiritual teachings, this deck shows us that the path to healing is not separate from faith but rather a profound expression of it.

In this way, the deck offers a sacred space for self-reflection, inviting us to explore our emotions, thoughts, and behaviors without judgment. It assures us that it's possible to hold both faith and self-awareness, using both to grow spiritually and emotionally.

A Journey Toward Spiritual Maturity

The Biblical Tarot: Shadows of the Soul is ultimately a guide on the journey to spiritual maturity. Just as biblical figures endured trials that tested their strength, humility, and devotion, this deck encourages us to face our own shadows to foster inner growth. By following this path, we develop a more profound sense of self and learn to align our actions with our highest values.

Spiritual maturity involves understanding and accepting all parts of ourselves, integrating our strengths with our shadows. The deck's Major Arcana cards serve as milestones on this journey, marking stages of transformation, challenges, and moments of divine insight. The Minor Arcana cards, with their focus on daily life, invite us to apply these lessons in small, everyday actions and choices. Together, these cards remind us that spiritual growth is not just about grand moments of enlightenment but also about the quieter, consistent efforts we make to be better each day.

Through this process, we learn to take accountability for our actions, forgive ourselves and others, and cultivate resilience in the face of adversity. Each card becomes a stepping stone, leading us closer to our authentic self. With every step, we gain the wisdom, compassion, and inner peace that define true spiritual maturity.

Chapter 23

How to Use the Biblical Tarot: Shadows of the Soul

The Biblical Tarot: Shadows of the Soul is a powerful tool for shadow work, guiding users through a journey of self-discovery, healing, and spiritual growth. To fully benefit from this deck, it's important to approach it with the right mindset, understanding, and intention. This chapter provides a comprehensive guide on how to work with the deck, from setting the stage and selecting spreads to interpreting the cards and integrating insights.

Setting the Right Mindset for Shadow Work

Before working with this deck, it's essential to cultivate a mindset of openness, courage, and humility. Shadow work is a journey into the parts of ourselves we often hide or ignore—our fears, insecurities, past traumas, and deep-seated emotions. These shadows can bring up uncomfortable memories and intense emotions, so approach each session with respect, patience, and a commitment to self-care.

Preparing Your Mind and Spirit: Shadow work can be transformative but requires mental and emotional strength. Take time to ground yourself, acknowledge that difficult emotions may arise, and remind yourself that this process is part of your healing and growth. Enter with a prayer, intention, or moment of silence, acknowledging that you are about to embark on an important spiritual journey.

The Importance of Reading the Book

Shadow work, when done intentionally and thoughtfully, has the power to illuminate hidden patterns, bring unresolved emotions to light, and help you integrate the aspects of yourself that you may have long avoided. The purpose of this deck, and the guidance provided in this book, is to support you in this process.

Before diving into the cards, it is highly recommended that you read the entire book. Understanding the structure, purpose, and intended use of the deck will provide a strong foundation for your journey. This background knowledge will also ensure that you approach shadow work with clarity, compassion, and respect for the process.

Creating a Sacred Space for Reflection

Working with the Biblical Tarot: Shadows of the Soul is a sacred practice. Prepare a quiet, comfortable space where you won't be disturbed. This space should feel safe and serene, allowing you to focus fully on your inner exploration.

- **Suggestions for a Sacred Space:** Consider lighting a candle, placing a Bible or other meaningful symbols nearby, and including a journal for reflections. Some may find it helpful to play calming music or use incense to create a peaceful atmosphere.

- **Setting an Intention:** Begin each session by setting a clear intention, such as "Reveal what needs healing" or "Help me understand my shadow." This intention will help guide the reading, providing a focused direction for the insights you receive.

Grounding Yourself Before You Begin

Shadow work can bring up intense emotions, hidden memories, or uncomfortable realizations. Grounding practices—such as taking a few deep breaths, visualizing roots connecting you to the earth, or saying a prayer—help anchor you in the present moment and prepare you to handle whatever arises with grace and strength.

Importance of Grounding: By grounding yourself, you build a stable foundation for facing the challenging emotions that may surface. This helps you stay balanced and prevents you from becoming overwhelmed by the intensity of shadow work.

Keeping an Open Mind and Heart

When using the Biblical Tarot for shadow work, approach each reading with an open mind. The insights you receive may surprise you or challenge your assumptions about yourself. By staying receptive, you allow for deeper self-awareness and understanding.

Importance of Openness: Resist the urge to judge or dismiss what the cards reveal. Instead, observe and reflect on how the insights resonate with your inner experiences. Growth comes from accepting all parts of yourself—the light and the shadow.

Shuffling and Connecting with the Cards

Connecting with the deck begins with shuffling the cards. As you shuffle, focus on your intention, allowing your energy to merge with the cards.

How to Shuffle: You may shuffle the traditional way, or spread the cards out and intuitively select them. Trust the process and let yourself be guided to the cards that hold the message you need.

Selecting a Spread for Shadow Work

The Biblical Tarot offers various spreads that serve different purposes. Below are some recommended spreads for shadow work, each suited to different levels of exploration.

- **Single-Card Reflection:** Draw a single card to gain a

  quick insight into a specific question or emotion. This is useful for daily reflections or simple guidance.

- **3-Card Spread for Shadow Work:**

  1. **The Hidden Shadow:** Reveals an unconscious or hidden part of your shadow.

2. **The Shadow's Influence:** Shows how this shadow affects your life and decisions.

3. **Path to Integration:** Offers guidance on embracing and transforming this shadow.

- **5-Card Spread for Inner Healing:**

  1. **Emotions:** What feelings need attention or healing.

  2. **Thoughts:** Insights into thoughts that may be limiting or empowering you.

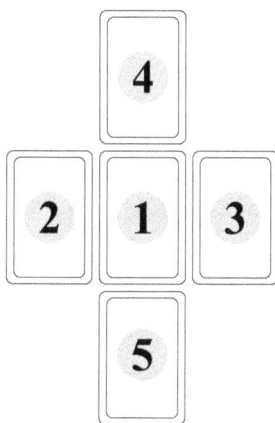

  3. **Behaviors:** Actions and habits influenced by the shadow.

  4. **Advice:** Guidance on moving forward.

  5. **Outcome:** Potential growth or healing that comes from addressing these shadows.

These spreads provide a structured approach to interpreting the messages of the cards and working through various layers of the shadow self.

Interpreting the Light and Shadow Aspects of Each Card

Each card in the Biblical Tarot: Shadows of the Soul has both light and shadow meanings, just as we each carry aspects of strength and vulnerability.

- **Light Aspect:** This represents the positive qualities, divine guidance, or spiritual potential within each card.

- **Shadow Aspect:** This side of the card reveals hidden fears, unresolved emotions, or challenges that hold you back.

For example, the Soul card may highlight the excitement of beginning a new journey in its light aspect but may also reflect naivety or avoidance of responsibility in its shadow aspect. Reflect on both aspects to gain a balanced understanding of each card's message.

Journal Prompts for Reflection

Journaling helps to deepen your insights and integrate the messages from your reading. After each session, write down the cards you drew, the insights you gained, and any thoughts or emotions that arose. This practice solidifies the learning and helps track your progress over time.

Sample Prompts:

- "What shadow did I uncover today, and how does it resonate with me?"

- "What emotions surfaced, and how can I begin to heal them?"

- "What guidance did I receive, and how can I apply it?"

Using Prayer or Meditation for Support

Prayer and meditation can be powerful tools for processing the insights gained from shadow work. After a reading, take a few moments to sit in silence, pray for guidance, or meditate on the messages you received. This allows time for the insights to settle and connects you to a higher source of wisdom.

Suggestions: Offer a prayer of gratitude, ask for strength to face difficult emotions, or spend a few minutes in quiet meditation to reflect on the reading.

Starting Slowly and Allowing Time for Healing

Shadow work can be intense, and it's important to pace yourself. Start with simple spreads and gradually move to more complex readings as you grow comfortable. Allow time between readings to process, reflect, and heal. Shadow work is a journey, not a race, and taking it slow helps prevent emotional overwhelm.

Closing a Reading with Gratitude and Reflection

Every reading is an opportunity for growth. End each session with gratitude, whether for the insights you gained or the strength to face difficult truths. Take a few deep breaths, thank yourself for doing this important work, and close the session with peace.

Chapter 24

Additional Spreads for Shadow Work

The Biblical Tarot: Shadows of the Soul was designed to guide spiritual seekers through the process of shadow work. The way the cards are laid out in a spread can influence how we interpret their messages and understand our inner journey. Different spreads offer varying levels of insight, depending on how deep you wish to go with your self-reflection.

Below are three suggested spreads—1-card, 3-card, and 5-card layouts—each offering a unique approach to unveiling and working through your shadows.

1-Card Spread: "The Light of Reflection"

Sometimes, simplicity offers the deepest insights. The 1-card spread is perfect for quick reflections or when you're focused on a specific aspect of your shadow work.

How to Use the 1-Card Spread:

Shuffle the deck while holding in mind a question or area of your shadow work where you need guidance. This could be as simple as asking, "What shadow do I need to confront today?"

Draw a single card from the deck and place it in front of you.

Reflect on the biblical story or character that the card represents. What lessons does the card offer about the shadow you're facing? Consider how the story ties into your life and what it reveals about the hidden aspects of yourself.

Example Questions for 1-Card Spread:

- "What shadow is blocking my personal growth right now?"

- "What message do I need to hear today about my inner struggles?"

The 1-card spread serves as a focused moment of reflection, helping you pinpoint the key area of your shadow work for the day.

3-Card Spread: "The Trinity of Shadows"

The 3-card spread offers a deeper dive, allowing you to explore how different aspects of your shadow interplay with each other. It helps illuminate past wounds, current challenges, and the potential for healing.

How to Use the 3-Card Spread:

Shuffle the deck with a specific intention in mind—perhaps you're looking to explore a pattern or habit that's been troubling you, or you want guidance on how to move past a personal blockage.

Draw three cards and place them in a line before you, from left to right.

Each card will represent a different aspect of your shadow work journey:

- **Card 1: *The Past Shadow*** - This card reveals a shadow from your past—an old wound, behavior, or emotion that you've carried with you. It asks, "What unresolved shadow from my past is still affecting me today?"

- **Card 2: *The Present Shadow*** - The second card speaks to the shadow you're currently wrestling with. It represents the hidden aspects of your present situation and asks, "What shadow am I currently facing or repressing?"

- **Card 3: *The Path to Integration*** - The final card offers guidance on how to heal and integrate the shadow. It provides a roadmap for transformation, asking, "How can I embrace and transform this shadow for personal growth?"

Example Questions for 3-Card Spread:

- "How can I better understand and heal a specific pattern of self-doubt?"

- "What shadow from my past is influencing my current relationships, and how can I release it?"

The 3-card spread offers a balanced view of your shadow work, helping you understand the origin of your shadow, its current impact, and how to move forward.

5-Card Spread: "The Journey into the Soul"

For those seeking an in-depth exploration of their shadow, the 5-card spread provides a full journey through the hidden aspects of the self, leading to profound insights and spiritual growth. This layout delves into the layers of your shadow, revealing the root cause, the current influence, and the path toward healing and transformation.

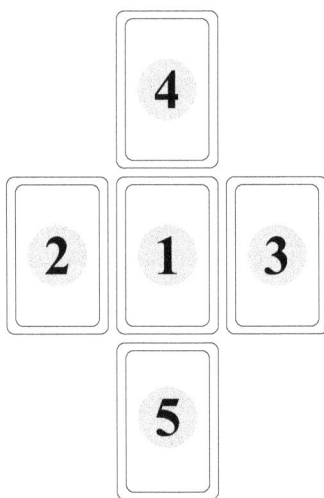

```
        ┌─────┐
        │  4  │
        └─────┘
┌─────┐ ┌─────┐ ┌─────┐
│  2  │ │  1  │ │  3  │
└─────┘ └─────┘ └─────┘
        ┌─────┐
        │  5  │
        └─────┘
```

How to Use this Spread:

Focus on a shadow that's been deeply troubling you—perhaps a persistent behavior, fear, or inner conflict.

Shuffle the deck with that intention in mind, asking for guidance through the process of integrating this shadow.

Draw five cards and lay them in the following positions:

- **Card 1:** The Shadow's Root
  This card reveals the origin of your shadow—where it began and why. It may relate to a specific experience, trauma, or unresolved emotion from your past.

- **Card 2:** How the Shadow Affects You
  The second card explores how this shadow manifests in your life. It asks, "What effect is this shadow having on my thoughts, behaviors, or relationships?"

- **Card 3:** The Divine Message
  This card brings in the biblical wisdom from Scripture. It offers a message from the Bible about how you can begin to confront or understand this shadow in light of your spiritual beliefs.

- **Card 4:** The Shadow's Lesson
  Every shadow carries a lesson for growth. This card asks, "What am I meant to learn from this shadow?" It helps you see how your shadow can be a source of personal development and insight.

- **Card 5:** The Path to Healing
  The final card provides guidance for healing and integrating your shadow. It offers a practical step forward, asking, "How can I bring this shadow into the light and allow it to transform me?"

Example Questions for this Spread:

- "What shadow from my past is hindering my spiritual growth, and how can I heal it?"

- "What lesson does this deep inner conflict hold for me, and how can I release it?"

The 5-card spread takes you on a journey into your soul, helping you uncover the hidden parts of yourself and guiding you through a transformative process of understanding, healing, and growth.

5-Card Spread: "The Mirror Within"

This spread is designed to reflect the hidden aspects of your psyche, providing clarity and insight into the shadow's influence on your life.

- **Card 1 - The Reflection:** What part of myself am I avoiding?

- **Card 2 - The Distortion:** What false beliefs or fears cloud my perception?

- **Card 3 - The Truth Revealed:** What lesson does my shadow hold for me?

- **Card 4 - The Integration:** How can I embrace and work with this shadow?

- **Card 5 - The Path Forward:** How will understanding this shadow transform my journey?

Example Questions:

- What hidden part of myself might hold the key to a recurring struggle?

- How can acknowledging this shadow help me unlock my potential?

5-Card Spread: "The Shadow's Voice"

This spread is an invitation to dialogue with your shadow, giving it space to express its needs and intentions.

- **Card 1 - The Call:** What is my shadow trying to tell me?

- **Card 2 - The Echo:** How has this shadow influenced my actions or relationships?

- **Card 3 - The Silence:** What part of me have I suppressed as a result?

- **Card 4 - The Response:** How can I honor and acknowledge this shadow?

- **Card 5 - The Harmony:** How can I create balance and peace with my shadow?

Example Questions:

- If my shadow could speak, what would it ask of me?

- How might listening to my shadow change the way I approach a current challenge?

5-Card Spread: "The Alchemy of the Soul"

This spread focuses on the transformative power of shadow work, helping you turn inner challenges into personal gold.

- **Card 1 - The Base Metal:** What unresolved pain or lim-

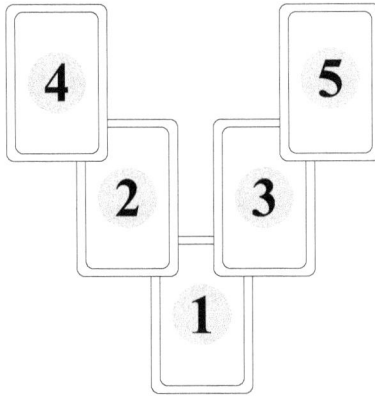

itation is surfacing?

- **Card 2 - The Fire:** What emotions or experiences are fueling this transformation?

- **Card 3 - The Crucible:** What part of myself is being tested or reshaped?

- **Card 4 - The Gold:** What new understanding or strength is emerging?

- **Card 5 - The Alchemist's Wisdom:** How can I apply this transformation in my life?

Example Questions:

- How can I turn my current challenges into opportunities for growth?

- What strength or wisdom might emerge from facing this shadow head-on?

5-Card Spread: "Jacob's Ladder – Ascending from Shadow to Light"

This spread is inspired by the biblical story of Jacob's Ladder, representing the connection between earthly struggles and divine wisdom. It guides the querent through the stages of shadow work, helping them ascend from the depths of their shadow to greater self-awareness and spiritual insight.

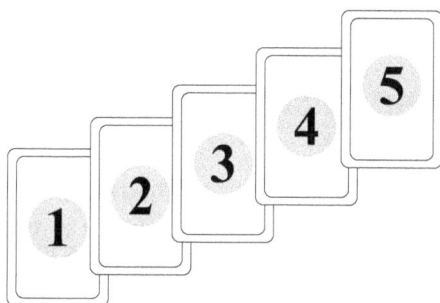

- **Card 1 - The Ground (Foundation):** What shadow aspect am I being called to confront?
  This card reveals the root of the current challenge or suppressed emotion that needs attention.

- **Card 2 - The Struggle (Climbing the Ladder):** What internal conflict is keeping me tethered?
  This card highlights the difficulties or resistance faced during the shadow work process.

- **Card 3 - The Angel (Guidance Along the Way):** What divine or intuitive wisdom can guide me through this? This card provides insight into the support, lessons, or resources available for navigating the shadow.

- **Card 4 - The Ascent (Progress Made):** How am I transforming through this process? This card reflects the personal growth and shifts occurring as you confront and integrate the shadow.

- **Card 5 - The Light (Divine Connection):** What higher understanding or purpose will emerge from this work? This card represents the spiritual or personal clarity gained through the journey.

Conclusion: Choosing the Right Spread

Each spread in the Biblical Tarot: Shadows of the Soul serves a different purpose, depending on where you are in your shadow work journey. Whether you're looking for a quick reflection, a balanced overview, or a deep dive into your soul's hidden corners, these spreads offer powerful tools to guide you through the process of embracing and transforming your shadows.

Remember, shadow work is a personal journey that takes time, courage, and patience. With each spread, you allow biblical wisdom to illuminate your path, helping you integrate the parts of yourself that have been hidden for too long.

Chapter 25

The Major Arcana:

Pathways of the Soul

The Major Arcana in the Biblical Tarot: Shadows of the Soul represents the profound journey of the soul through the universal cycles of growth, transformation, and spiritual awakening. Each of the 22 cards is a portal into a pivotal moment in human experience, illuminated by a biblical story that reflects the card's deeper truths. These cards embody the grand archetypes of life—love, faith, challenge, redemption, and wisdom—revealing the divine patterns that guide our spiritual evolution.

From the creation of a living being (The Soul) to the ultimate harmony of the New Jerusalem (The World), the Major Arcana charts the soul's sacred pilgrimage. It serves as a mirror for life's most significant lessons, inviting us to confront our shadows, embrace our inner light, and discover the divine within. These cards are not merely symbols but sacred signposts, guiding seekers through the labyrinth of shadow work toward wholeness, freedom, and spiritual maturity.

The Soul

CREATION OF A LIVING BEING

*Then the LORD God formed man from the dust of the ground
and breathed the breath of life into his nostrils,
and the man became a living being.*
Genesis 2:7 BSB

THE SOUL
CREATION OF A LIVING BEING (GENESIS 2:7)

The concept of "The Soul" as the initial creation of a living being reflects this card's themes of beginnings and untapped potential. In the biblical narrative, the soul's creation marks the start of humanity's journey, imbued with divine breath and the freedom to choose its path. This moment of creation represents purity, innocence, and the nascent stage of spiritual and existential exploration, akin to the stepping out into the unknown.

UPRIGHT KEYWORDS:	REVERSED KEYWORDS:
Beginnings	Naivety
Innocence	Lack of Direction
Potential	Impulsiveness
Freedom	Missed Opportunities
Leap of Faith	Wrong Choices

Upright: The journey of shadow work begins with The Soul, representing a leap into the unknown. Shadow work requires innocence and openness as we step into the process of self-discovery. We must acknowledge our hidden potential and allow ourselves to explore new, uncharted territories of the psyche. This card signals the beginning of the soul's journey toward transformation.

- **Beginnings** – Initiating your journey into self-discovery and shadow work.
- **Innocence** – Approaching your inner world with purity and openness.
- **Potential** – Recognizing the limitless possibilities within yourself.
- **Freedom** – Embracing free will to explore and transform your shadows.
- **Leap of Faith** – Trusting the process despite uncertainties and fears.

Reversed: In the shadow aspect, The Soul can represent fear of self-exploration. It shows a reluctance to embark on the journey, leading to impulsive decisions or avoidance. This card asks you to consider the missed opportunities that arise when we resist facing our deeper selves.

- **Naivety** – Acting without fully understanding the depth of your shadow.
- **Lack of Direction** – Feeling lost or unsure about your path in shadow work.
- **Impulsiveness** – Making hasty decisions that hinder your healing process.
- **Missed Opportunities** – Failing to seize chances for deeper self-exploration.
- **Wrong Choices** – Taking actions that lead away from personal growth.

The Magician

MOSES

Then Moses stretched out his hand over the sea,
and all that night the LORD drove back the sea with a strong east
wind that turned it into dry land. So the waters were divided
Exodus 14:21 BSB

Moses is a central figure in the Bible, renowned for leading the Israelites out of Egyptian bondage and towards the Promised Land. His life story is one of transformation, from a humble beginning to becoming a great leader and intermediary between God and the Israelites. Moses's act of splitting the sea represents the pinnacle of his faith and divine empowerment, making him an embodiment of The Magician's ability to harness resources and will to create miracles.

UPRIGHT KEYWORDS:	REVERSED KEYWORDS:
Mastery	Self-Doubt
Wisdom	Misuse of Power
Resourcefulness	Lack of Direction
Adaptability	Hesitancy
Transformation	Misunderstanding

Upright: The Magician represents mastery over the self, showing that shadow work requires the inner strength to confront hidden fears and traumas. It signifies that you have the tools to transform your shadow into light, using wisdom and resourcefulness. Like Moses, it reflects the capacity for spiritual leadership and transformation.

- **Mastery** – Harnessing your abilities to transform and integrate your shadow.
- **Wisdom** – Guiding your shadow work with deep insight and understanding.
- **Resourcefulness** – Utilizing available tools to navigate inner challenges.
- **Adaptability** – Adjusting your approach as you confront deeper issues.
- **Transformation** – Manifesting positive change through self-discovery.

Reversed: When reversed, The Magician reflects the misuse of personal power or self-doubt. Shadow work may be stalled due to a lack of belief in one's abilities. The shadow here shows that you may be hesitating to confront deeper issues, allowing unresolved aspects to fester.

- **Self-Doubt** – Questioning your ability to handle the complexities of shadow work.
- **Misuse of Power** – Allowing control issues to hinder your healing process.
- **Lack of Direction** – Feeling lost in your self-discovery journey.
- **Hesitancy** – Reluctance to take necessary actions for personal growth.
- **Misunderstanding** – Misinterpreting the meanings of your insights and emotions.

The High Priestess

MARY MAGDALENE

Early on the first day of the week, after Jesus had risen,
He appeared first to Mary Magdalene,
from whom He had driven out seven demons.
Mark 16:9 BSB

THE HIGH PRIESTESS
MARY MAGDALENE

Mary Magdalene is a significant figure in the New Testament, often depicted as a close follower of Jesus. Seven demons had been driven out of her, and this is why shy is portrayed with seven skulls below her on the card. Seven refers symbolically to "completeness" – the total cure of all evil. Her story is a testament to personal transformation and redemption. Mary Magdalene's journey from darkness to being a witness to the resurrection embodies the themes of accessing deep, inner knowledge and the balance between seen and unseen worlds.

UPRIGHT KEYWORDS:	REVERSED KEYWORDS:
Intuition	Suppressed Intuition
Mystery	Hidden Truths
Wisdom	Emotional Turmoil
Reflection	Unrealized Potential
Transformation	Worldly Temptations

Upright: The High Priestess embodies spiritual insight and intuition, vital tools for shadow work. It calls for introspection and connecting with the mysteries within, trusting that the unknown parts of the self can lead to profound healing. She encourages the seeker to face buried truths with grace and dignity.

- **Intuition** – Trusting your inner voice to guide your shadow work.

- **Mystery** – Embracing the unknown aspects of your subconscious.

- **Wisdom** – Gaining deep spiritual insights through introspection.

- **Reflection** – Contemplating your hidden truths and emotions.

- **Transformation** – Undergoing profound inner changes through self-awareness.

Reversed: In reverse, this card points to suppressed intuition and the inability to see what lies beneath. There is a blockage preventing deep self-reflection, indicating a resistance to confronting difficult emotions or shadow aspects. It's a sign that one's inner wisdom is being ignored, leading to emotional imbalance.

- **Suppressed Intuition** – Ignoring or denying your inner guidance.

- **Hidden Truths** – Keeping unresolved issues buried within.

- **Emotional Turmoil** – Experiencing imbalance due to ignored feelings.

- **Unrealized Potential** – Failing to unlock deeper aspects of yourself.

- **Worldly Temptations** – Succumbing to distractions that divert from inner healing.

The Empress

MARY, MOTHER OF JESUS

The angel replied, "The Holy Spirit will come upon you,
and the power of the Most High will overshadow you.
So the Holy One to be born will be called the Son of God.
Luke 1:35 BSB

Mary, the mother of Jesus, is a central figure in Christianity, revered for her obedience, faith, and role in the divine plan of salvation. Her acceptance of her role, despite the challenges, exemplifies unconditional love, nurturing, and the birthing of new ideas and spiritual paths. Mary's journey embodies the essence of The Empress, representing fertility, creativity, and the nurturing of life and faith.

UPRIGHT KEYWORDS:	REVERSED KEYWORDS:
Nurturing	Over-Protectiveness
Creation	Neglect
Gentleness	Emotional Dependency
Emotional Depth	Blocked Creativity
Protection	Disconnection

Upright: The Empress brings nurturing and healing energy to shadow work. It invites you to embrace your emotional depth, offering love and comfort to the parts of yourself that have been wounded. Through nurturing the inner child and cultivating self-compassion, you find the strength to heal.

- **Nurturing** – Providing care and compassion to your wounded self.
- **Creation** – Cultivating new aspects of your identity through shadow work.
- **Gentleness** – Approaching your inner wounds with softness and kindness.
- **Emotional Depth** – Delving into profound feelings for healing.
- **Protection** – Safeguarding your emotional well-being during transformation.

Reversed: The reversed Empress suggests neglect of self-care or a disconnection from your emotions. It may point to overprotectiveness or emotional dependency, blocking your ability to face and integrate your shadow. Creativity and emotional flow are stifled when these aspects are left unacknowledged.

- **Over-Protectiveness** – Smothering yourself or others, hindering growth.
- **Neglect** – Ignoring your own self-care needs.
- **Emotional Dependency** – Relying too heavily on others for emotional support.
- **Blocked Creativity** – Stifling your ability to express and transform.
- **Disconnection** – Losing touch with your intuitive and emotional self.

The Emperor

KING SOLOMON

...behold, I will do what you have asked. I will give you a wise and discerning heart, so that there will never have been another like you, nor will there ever be.
1 Kings 3:12 BSB

THE EMPEROR
KING SOLOMON

King Solomon, son of David and Bathsheba, was the third king of Israel. His reign is often considered Israel's golden age, marked by peace, prosperity, and architectural achievements, including the building of the First Temple in Jerusalem. Solomon is most renowned for his wisdom, granted by God in response to his prayer for an understanding heart to judge his people fairly. His story encapsulates the balance of power, wisdom, and justice, embodying The Emperor's essence.

UPRIGHT KEYWORDS:	REVERSED KEYWORDS:
Authority	Abuse of Power
Wisdom	Poor Judgment
Leadership	Materialism
Stability	Injustice
Accomplishment	Neglect

Upright: The Emperor represents authority and structure in shadow work. It encourages you to approach inner conflicts with discipline, applying wisdom and discernment to confront your shadow. This card speaks of building strong foundations through introspection and conscious choices.

- **Authority** – Establishing control over your shadow work process.

- **Wisdom** – Applying discerning judgment to your inner conflicts.

- **Leadership** – Guiding yourself with strength and purpose.

- **Stability** – Building a solid foundation for personal growth.

- **Accomplishment** – Achieving significant milestones in your healing journey.

Reversed: In its shadow form, The Emperor can indicate a misuse of personal power, where ego or control blocks the ability to grow. You may find yourself being too rigid, using authority to suppress rather than face your shadow. It calls for balance between strength and vulnerability.

- **Abuse of Power** – Misusing control to suppress your shadow.

- **Poor Judgment** – Making decisions that impede your healing.

- **Materialism** – Overemphasizing material stability at the expense of emotional growth.

- **Injustice** – Experiencing unfairness in your internal conflicts.

- **Neglect** – Failing to take responsibility for your personal development.

The High Priest

AARON, BROTHER OF MOSES

"...You must distinguish between the holy and the common,
between the clean and the unclean,
so that you may teach the Israelites all the statutes
that the LORD has given them through Moses."
Leviticus 10:10-11 BSB

THE HIGH PRIEST
AARON BROTHER OF MOSES

Aaron, as Moses' brother and the first high priest of Israel, played a critical role in the establishment and maintenance of the Israelite's religious practices and traditions. He was a key figure in communicating God's laws and performing sacred rituals, embodying the qualities of spiritual leadership, guidance, and tradition. Aaron's life illustrates the complexities of adhering to divine will while facing the challenges of leadership and faith.

UPRIGHT KEYWORDS:	REVERSED KEYWORDS:
Spiritual Guidance	Rigidity
Tradition	Rebellion
Rituals	Misuse of Authority
Mentorship	Loss of Faith
Community	Hypocrisy

Upright: The High Priest represents spiritual mentorship in shadow work, offering guidance as you delve into your subconscious. This card emphasizes the importance of tradition and spiritual practices in confronting and integrating hidden aspects of the self.

- **Spiritual Guidance** – Receiving mentorship in your shadow work.
- **Tradition** – Honoring established practices in your healing process.
- **Rituals** – Utilizing spiritual ceremonies to confront your shadow.
- **Mentorship** – Seeking wisdom from trusted spiritual advisors.
- **Community** – Finding strength in collective support during self-discovery.

Reversed: When reversed, it reflects a rigid attachment to dogma, preventing true self-exploration. It can indicate a loss of spiritual direction, rebellion against inner truths, or misuse of spiritual authority to avoid personal growth.

- **Rigidity** – Being overly dogmatic, hindering flexible healing.
- **Rebellion** – Rejecting traditional methods of shadow work.
- **Misuse of Authority** – Letting spiritual leaders control rather than guide.
- **Loss of Faith** – Feeling disconnected from your spiritual path.
- **Hypocrisy** – Exhibiting dishonesty in your spiritual practices.

The Lovers

ADAM AND EVE

And Adam named his wife Eve,
because she would be the mother of all the living.
Genesis 3:20 BSB

Adam and Eve, according to the Bible, were the first humans created by God and placed in the Garden of Eden. Their story is foundational, illustrating themes of love, choice, temptation, and the consequences of their actions. Their decision to eat from the Tree of Knowledge, leading to their expulsion from Eden, highlights the complexities of free will, temptation, and the pursuit of wisdom at the cost of harmony.

UPRIGHT KEYWORDS:	REVERSED KEYWORDS:
Union	Disharmony
Choices	Poor Decisions
Harmony	Loss of Innocence
Temptation	Yielding to Temptation
Awakening	Isolation

Upright: The Lovers represents the choices you make during shadow work, especially those relating to inner conflict between light and shadow. It calls for balance and integration of dualities, suggesting that through embracing both good and difficult aspects of yourself, you experience personal awakening.

- **Union** – Harmonizing conflicting aspects within yourself.
- **Choices** – Making conscious decisions about your shadow integration.
- **Harmony** – Achieving balance between light and dark within.
- **Temptation** – Facing moral and ethical challenges in shadow work.
- **Awakening** – Gaining deeper self-awareness through inner conflicts.

Reversed: The reversed Lovers signifies disharmony, poor decisions, and inner conflict. It suggests yielding to temptation or denying the shadow. There may be a disconnect between who you are and who you think you should be, causing emotional disarray.

- **Disharmony** – Experiencing internal conflict and imbalance.
- **Poor Decisions** – Making choices that hinder your healing.
- **Loss of Innocence** – Confronting painful truths about yourself.
- **Yielding to Temptation** – Succumbing to negative influences instead of resisting.
- **Isolation** – Feeling disconnected from your integrated self.

The Chariot

PHARAOH'S PURSUIT

And the Egyptians chased after them — all Pharaoh's horses,
chariots, and horsemen — and followed them into the sea.
Exodus 14:23 BSB

THE CHARIOT
PHARAOH'S PURSUIT (EXODUS 14)

In the context of the Exodus story, Pharaoh represents the epitome of earthly power and opposition to the will of God, as manifested through Moses and the Israelites' quest for freedom. His decision to pursue the Israelites with chariots symbolizes a direct confrontation with divine will, embodying the struggle between control and surrender.

UPRIGHT KEYWORDS:	REVERSED KEYWORDS:
Determination	Overbearing Control
Willpower	Loss of Direction
Control	Defeat
Conflict	Uncontrolled Aggression
Direction	Ethical Consequences

Upright: The Chariot symbolizes determination and willpower in confronting your shadow. It indicates that you have the strength to drive forward in your shadow work, using self-control to navigate internal conflict. It represents the movement toward integrating your hidden aspects.

- **Determination** – Moving forward with resolve in your shadow work.
- **Willpower** – Harnessing your inner strength to confront challenges.
- **Control** – Managing conflicting emotions with discipline.
- **Conflict** – Engaging with internal struggles to achieve balance.
- **Direction** – Steering your healing journey with clear intent.

Reversed: In reverse, The Chariot warns of being overly controlling or aggressive in your shadow work, leading to resistance. There is a loss of direction, and inner conflict becomes overwhelming rather than transformative. You may be struggling with unchecked emotions or ethical dilemmas.

- **Overbearing Control** – Letting excessive force disrupt your healing.
- **Loss of Direction** – Feeling aimless in your shadow integration.
- **Defeat** – Experiencing setbacks in your personal growth.
- **Uncontrolled Aggression** – Letting anger hinder your healing process.
- **Ethical Consequences** – Facing moral dilemmas that complicate your journey.

Strength

DANIEL IN THE LION'S DEN

"...My God sent His angel and shut the mouths of the lions. They have not hurt me, for I was found innocent in His sight, and I have done no wrong against you, O king."
Daniel 6:22 BSB

Daniel, a Jewish prophet, blessed by God with the wisdom and ability to interpret dreams, is known for his unwavering faith, even when faced with death. His story illustrates his moral and spiritual strength. Despite being thrown into the den as punishment for praying to God (against the king's decree), Daniel's faith protected him, and he emerged unscathed. His integrity and trust in divine power make him a perfect embodiment of the Strength card's themes.

UPRIGHT KEYWORDS:	REVERSED KEYWORDS:
Courage	Fear
Resilience	Doubt
Faith	Loss of Control
Emotional Control	Weakness
Integrity	Compromised Integrity

Upright: Strength represents inner courage and moral integrity, reminding you that shadow work requires you to face fears with grace. Like Daniel, you must trust in your own resilience and the strength of your spirit to overcome the challenges of integrating your shadow.

- **Courage** – Facing your fears with bravery during shadow work.
- **Resilience** – Maintaining composure under emotional pressure.
- **Faith** – Trusting in your spiritual strength to overcome challenges.
- **Emotional Control** – Managing your fears and emotions effectively.
- **Integrity** – Upholding your moral values in the healing process.

Reversed: When reversed, this card reveals fear, doubt, and loss of control over your emotions. It suggests that you are struggling to tame your inner "lions" and feel overwhelmed by the intensity of shadow work.

- **Fear** – Letting anxiety impede your shadow work.
- **Doubt** – Questioning your ability to handle emotional challenges.
- **Loss of Control** – Struggling to manage your emotions.
- **Weakness** – Feeling powerless against your inner conflicts.
- **Compromised Integrity** – Allowing fears to lead you away from your values.

The Hermit

JOHN THE BAPTIST

This is he who was spoken of through the prophet Isaiah:
"A voice of one calling in the wilderness,
'Prepare the way for the Lord,
make straight paths for Him.'"
Matthew 3:3 BSB

THE HERMIT
JOHN THE BAPTIST

John the Baptist is a pivotal figure in the New Testament, known for his ascetic lifestyle in the wilderness and his role in baptizing Jesus. His life was marked by deep spiritual commitment, reflection, and the calling to prepare others for the coming of the Messiah.

John's dedication to his faith, despite societal detachment, embodies the themes of seeking wisdom in solitude and guiding others on their spiritual journey.

UPRIGHT KEYWORDS:	REVERSED KEYWORDS:
Enlightenment	Isolation
Introspection	Lost Path
Guidance	Reluctance
Preparation	Confusion
Devotion	Withdrawal

Upright: The Hermit signifies the need for solitude and reflection during shadow work. It encourages deep introspection and self-guidance, as you journey inward to uncover hidden aspects of yourself. This card represents wisdom gained through spiritual solitude.

- **Enlightenment** – Gaining deep spiritual insights through solitude.
- **Introspection** – Reflecting deeply on your inner self.
- **Guidance** – Seeking inner wisdom to navigate your shadow work.
- **Preparation** – Preparing mentally and spiritually for transformation.
- **Devotion** – Committing yourself to the healing journey with dedication.

Reversed: In reverse, it suggests isolation or reluctance to engage with your shadow. It warns against withdrawing too deeply or becoming lost in introspection without taking action. There is a risk of missing the insights needed for growth.

- **Isolation** – Feeling lonely or disconnected from others in your healing.
- **Lost Path** – Struggling to find direction in your shadow work.
- **Reluctance** – Avoiding deep introspection and reflection.
- **Confusion** – Experiencing unclear insights or misguided thoughts.
- **Withdrawal** – Excessively retreating from the world, hindering growth.

Wheel of Life

CYCLES OF LIFE

For everything there is a season,
and a time for every purpose under heaven
Ecclesiastes 3:1 BSB

This card doesn't focus on a single character, but rather on the universal experience shared by all of humanity as depicted in the Bible. It acknowledges the seasons of life, the rise and fall of nations, and the personal journeys of faith, hardship, and redemption. It depicts the cyclical nature of human experiences, the inevitability of change, and the guiding hand of destiny or divine will.

This theme reflects the ongoing dance of creation and renewal echoed throughout the Bible.

UPRIGHT KEYWORDS:	REVERSED KEYWORDS:
Change	Helplessness
Interconnectedness	Resistance
Hope	Disconnection
Guidance	Chaos
Fate	Misinterpretation

Upright: The Wheel of Life symbolizes the cycles of transformation inherent in shadow work. It reminds you that change is constant and that confronting your shadow is part of life's natural ebb and flow. It brings hope and divine guidance, showing that each phase has a purpose.

- **Change** – Embracing the natural cycles of transformation in shadow work.
- **Interconnectedness** – Understanding how events and emotions are linked.
- **Hope** – Maintaining optimism through periods of change.
- **Guidance** – Trusting in divine providence during your healing journey.
- **Fate** – Acknowledging the role of destiny in your personal growth.

Reversed: When reversed, this card points to resistance to change and a feeling of helplessness in the face of life's challenges. It suggests a disconnect from the divine and a reluctance to engage in the natural process of growth.

- **Helplessness** – Feeling powerless against the changes in your life.
- **Resistance** – Struggling to accept necessary transformations.
- **Disconnection** – Losing faith in divine guidance or support.
- **Chaos** – Experiencing disorder and lack of direction in your healing.
- **Misinterpretation** – Misunderstanding the signs and events in your journey.

Justice

THE TEN COMMANDMENTS

*You must walk in all the ways that the LORD your God has
commanded you, so that you may live and prosper
and prolong your days in the land that you will possess.*
Deuteronomy 5:33 BSB

The Ten Commandments were given to Moses by God on Mount Sinai and represent God's laws for His people, Israel. They encompass duties to God and to fellow humans, laying down a framework for justice, respect, and ethical conduct.

The commandments are fundamental to the Judeo-Christian moral and legal systems, symbolizing the divine origin of justice and the importance of living in accordance with divine and moral law.

UPRIGHT KEYWORDS:	REVERSED KEYWORDS:
Fairness	Injustice
Truth	Dishonesty
Accountability	Imbalance
Balance	Avoidance
Integrity	Karmic Debt

Upright: Justice represents fairness, truth, and balance in shadow work. It calls you to examine your actions, thoughts, and behaviors with honesty and integrity. This card signifies that shadow work requires taking responsibility for both light and dark aspects of the self, seeking a balanced and fair perspective. You are asked to confront the consequences of past actions and to make amends where necessary.

- **Fairness** – Seeking balanced and unbiased judgments in shadow work.
- **Truth** – Confronting and embracing the truth about yourself.
- **Accountability** – Taking responsibility for your actions and their impacts.
- **Balance** – Harmonizing opposing aspects of your inner self.
- **Integrity** – Upholding moral principles during your healing process.

Reversed: The reversed Justice card points to dishonesty, avoidance of responsibility, or imbalance in your shadow work. There may be a refusal to confront certain truths about yourself or a tendency to blame others rather than taking ownership of your actions. It suggests that inner work is being stalled due to a lack of accountability.

- **Injustice** – Experiencing unfairness or bias in your self-assessment.
- **Dishonesty** – Avoiding the truth about your shadow aspects.
- **Imbalance** – Failing to harmonize conflicting emotions or thoughts.
- **Avoidance** – Refusing to take responsibility for your actions.
- **Karmic Debt** – Accumulating unresolved issues due to lack of accountability.

The Hanged Man

PETER'S CRUCIFIXION

Then Jesus said to all of them,
"If anyone wants to come after Me, he must deny himself and take
up his cross daily and follow Me. For whoever wants to save his life
will lose it, but whoever loses his life for My sake will save it.
Luke 9:23-24 BSB

THE HANGED MAN
PETER'S CRUCIFIXION (ACTS OF PETER)

Peter, one of Jesus' closest disciples, is a foundational figure in Christianity. Known for his bold faith and, at times, his impetuousness, Peter's journey with Jesus includes moments of profound insight and human frailty. His eventual martyrdom, according to tradition, symbolizes ultimate faithfulness and humility, choosing to be crucified upside down because he did not see himself as equal to Jesus. Peter's story is a testament to personal transformation and the power of faith.

UPRIGHT KEYWORDS:	REVERSED KEYWORDS:
Surrender	Stagnation
Perspective Shift	Fear of Sacrifice
Sacrifice	Limited Perspective
Patience	Spiritual Disconnect
Transformation	Ego Control

Upright: The Hanged Man signifies surrender, sacrifice, and a shift in perspective. In shadow work, it represents the need to let go of old patterns and beliefs that no longer serve you. This card suggests a period of spiritual surrender, where you are asked to release control and trust in the transformative power of letting go. It encourages seeing your shadows from a new angle, allowing for deeper insight and healing.

- **Surrender** – Letting go of control to facilitate healing.
- **Perspective Shift** – Viewing your shadow from a new angle.
- **Sacrifice** – Releasing old patterns that hinder your growth.
- **Patience** – Waiting through difficult phases with trust.
- **Transformation** – Embracing change through voluntary surrender.

Reversed: In this position, this card points to resistance to change, refusal to surrender, or feeling stuck in the shadow work process. It may indicate that you are holding on too tightly to old habits or thought patterns, preventing true growth and transformation. This card asks you to reconsider your approach and release what is no longer serving your highest good.

- **Stagnation** – Resisting necessary changes and remaining stuck.
- **Fear of Sacrifice** – Unwillingness to let go of old patterns.
- **Limited Perspective** – Failing to see your shadow from different angles.
- **Spiritual Disconnect** – Losing faith in the transformative process.
- **Ego Control** – Letting pride interfere with your healing journey.

Death

THE FOURTH HORSEMAN

And behold, a pale horse,
and the name of he who sat on it was Death.
Revelation 6:8 WEB

The fourth horseman of the apocalypse, as described in the Book of Revelation, is a symbolic figure representing death and the profound changes that follow in its wake. Accompanied by Hades, the horseman is granted power to bring about death through various means, symbolizing the inevitable and transformative nature of end times. This character underscores the theme of inevitable change and the cycle of life and death.

UPRIGHT KEYWORDS:	REVERSED KEYWORDS:
Transformation	Resistance to Change
Renewal	Fear of the Unknown
Release	Stagnation
Endings	Unfinished Business
Rebirth	Delayed Transformation

Upright: The Death card symbolizes transformation and the end of a cycle. In shadow work, it represents the death of old ways of being and the release of what no longer serves you. This card marks the end of a difficult chapter, making way for personal renewal and growth. Embrace the necessary endings in your life so that new beginnings can take root.

- **Transformation** – Embracing the end of old ways to foster growth.
- **Renewal** – Beginning a new chapter after significant change.
- **Release** – Letting go of past traumas and limiting beliefs.
- **Endings** – Concluding old cycles to make way for new beginnings.
- **Rebirth** – Emerging renewed and stronger after facing your shadow.

Reversed: When reversed, Death suggests fear of change and resistance to transformation. It indicates a clinging to the past or a reluctance to let go of familiar patterns, even if they are harmful. Shadow work is being blocked by a refusal to release old identities or attachments.

- **Resistance to Change** – Clinging to the past and fearing transformation.
- **Fear of the Unknown** – Avoiding the necessary end of old patterns.
- **Stagnation** – Remaining stuck in old cycles without progress.
- **Unfinished Business** – Leaving unresolved issues that hinder healing.
- **Delayed Transformation** – Postponing the necessary changes for growth.

Temperance

MARY AND MARTHA

Jesus answered her,
"Martha, Martha, you are anxious and troubled about many
things, but one thing is needed. Mary has chosen the good part,
which will not be taken away from her."
Luke 10:41-42 WEB

Mary and Martha, sisters of Lazarus, offer contrasting approaches to Jesus' visit. Martha is preoccupied with the hospitality duties, stressing over the details of serving their guest, while Mary chooses to sit at Jesus' feet, listening to his teachings. This story contrasts the active service and spiritual attentiveness, embodying the Temperance card's call for balance between worldly responsibilities and spiritual well-being.

UPRIGHT KEYWORDS:	REVERSED KEYWORDS:
Balance	Imbalance
Moderation	Overindulgence
Harmony	Neglect
Patience	Conflict
Inner Peace	Distracted Focus

Upright: Temperance symbolizes balance, moderation, and harmony. In shadow work, this card encourages you to approach your inner journey with patience and calm, blending opposing forces within yourself to create inner peace. Temperance reflects the alchemical process of transforming emotions, thoughts, and energies into something greater. It calls for measured reflection and emotional regulation as you navigate your shadows.

- **Balance** – Harmonizing conflicting emotions and thoughts.
- **Moderation** – Practicing self-control in your healing process.
- **Harmony** – Creating inner peace through integration of your shadow.
- **Patience** – Allowing time for gradual healing and transformation.
- **Inner Peace** – Achieving calmness through balanced emotional states.

Reversed: Reversed, Temperance suggests imbalance, excess, or lack of harmony in your approach to shadow work. It indicates extremes—either overindulgence in the exploration of the self or avoidance of the process altogether. The key lesson here is to restore balance by practicing moderation and aligning your actions with your inner wisdom.

- **Imbalance** – Experiencing emotional turmoil and lack of harmony.
- **Overindulgence** – Excessive behavior that disrupts your healing.
- **Neglect** – Ignoring your spiritual and emotional needs.
- **Conflict** – Facing discord within yourself or in relationships.
- **Distracted Focus** – Losing sight of your healing goals due to overwhelm.

The Devil

SATAN TEMPTING HUMANS TO SIN

But each one is tempted when by his own evil desires he is lured away and enticed. Then after desire has conceived, it gives birth to sin; and sin, when it is full-grown, gives birth to death.
James 1:14-15 BSB

Satan, often depicted as a fallen angel, embodies the ultimate tempter or adversary in Christian theology. He is known for his cunning ability to deceive, seduce, and lead humans away from divine will, enticing them into actions that bind them to the material world or their own shadows, away from spiritual truth.

UPRIGHT KEYWORDS:	REVERSED KEYWORDS:
Temptation	Liberation
Addiction	Awareness
Bondage	Resisting Temptation
Control	Releasing Control
Fear	Empowerment

Upright: The Devil represents the darker aspects of the self, including temptation, addiction, and unhealthy attachments. In shadow work, it confronts the shadow directly, asking you to examine where you are giving away your power to negative influences. You are being tested whether you can resist temptation and overcome the shadows that seek to bind you. This card calls for self-awareness, courage, and the willingness to confront your darkest fears.

- **Temptation** – Confronting the allure of unhealthy habits and behaviors.
- **Addiction** – Recognizing and addressing dependencies that bind you.
- **Bondage** – Identifying the ways you are trapped by negative patterns.
- **Control** – Acknowledging external or internal forces that limit your freedom.
- **Fear** – Facing the fears that prevent you from embracing your true self.

Reversed: Upside down, The Devil represents liberation from bondage and breaking free from destructive patterns. It signals a release of unhealthy attachments, addictions, or fears that have held you captive. Shadow work is leading to a powerful transformation, where you are reclaiming your personal power and shedding the chains of self-limiting beliefs.

- **Liberation** – Breaking free from unhealthy attachments and dependencies.
- **Awareness** – Gaining insight into the forces that control you.
- **Resisting Temptation** – Strengthening your ability to reject negative influences.
- **Releasing Control** – Letting go of the need to dominate your shadow.
- **Empowerment** – Reclaiming your personal power and autonomy.

The Tower

TOWER OF BABEL

"Come," they said, "let us build for ourselves a city with a tower that reaches to the heavens, that we may make a name for ourselves and not be scattered over the face of all the earth."
Genesis 11:4 BSB

The Tower of Babel story from Genesis describes humanity's united effort to build a tower tall enough to reach heaven. This act of pride and ambition led God to confuse their language, making them unable to communicate and cooperate, which resulted in the scattering of people across the earth and the abandonment of the tower. This narrative serves as a reminder of the potential consequences of human hubris and the disruptive power of divine will.

UPRIGHT KEYWORDS:	REVERSED KEYWORDS:
Disruption	Resistance to Change
Collapse	Delayed Reckoning
Chaos	Fear of Disaster
Forced Change	Internal Upheaval
Revelation	Avoidance

Upright: The Tower represents sudden change, upheaval, and the breaking down of false structures. In shadow work, this card symbolizes a dramatic revelation or realization that shakes the foundation of your beliefs and identity. Like the Tower of Babel, the structures you have built around your shadow may come crashing down, forcing you to face difficult truths. This card invites you to embrace the chaos as a necessary part of growth and transformation, clearing the way for rebuilding a more authentic self.

- **Disruption** – Experiencing sudden changes that challenge your foundations.

- **Collapse** – Letting go of false structures that no longer serve you.

- **Chaos** – Navigating through turmoil to achieve clarity.

- **Forced Change** – Embracing necessary transformations that arise from upheaval.

- **Revelation** – Gaining truth through the breakdown of illusions.

Reversed: Reversed, The Tower suggests that you may be resisting change or attempting to hold on to crumbling structures in your life. It indicates a refusal to face the truths that shadow work is bringing to light, resulting in prolonged suffering. This card warns that delaying the inevitable only prolongs the difficulty of the transformation process.

- **Resistance to Change** – Avoiding necessary upheavals that lead to growth.

- **Delayed Reckoning** – Postponing the confrontation with your shadow.

- **Fear of Disaster** – Letting fear prevent you from embracing transformation.

- **Internal Upheaval** – Experiencing turmoil within without external cause.

- **Avoidance** – Refusing to face the truths that require change.

The Star

STAR OF BETHLEHEM

After Jesus was born in Bethlehem in Judea, during the time of King Herod, Magi from the east arrived in Jerusalem, asking, "Where is the One who has been born King of the Jews? We saw His star in the east and have come to worship Him."
Matthew 2:1-2 BSB

The Star of Bethlehem is a celestial phenomenon mentioned in the Gospel of Matthew, associated with the birth of Jesus Christ. It is described as leading the Magi (wise men) from the East to Jerusalem to celebrate the birth of the "king of the Jews."

The star symbolizes divine intervention in the world and the manifestation of prophecy, guiding those who seek enlightenment and truth.

UPRIGHT KEYWORDS:	REVERSED KEYWORDS:
Hope	Loss of Faith
Guidance	Confusion
Renewal	Despair
Clarity	Lack of Inspiration
Faith	Inner Turmoil

Upright: The Star symbolizes hope, faith, and divine guidance. In shadow work, this card represents a moment of spiritual clarity and renewal after a period of darkness. It reflects the light at the end of the tunnel, offering reassurance that the hard work of confronting your shadow will lead to healing and blessings. It encourages you to trust in the process and follow your inner light toward wholeness.

- **Hope** – Maintaining optimism through the healing journey.
- **Guidance** – Receiving spiritual insights that lead to clarity.
- **Renewal** – Experiencing rejuvenation after facing your shadows.
- **Clarity** – Gaining clear understanding of your emotional landscape.
- **Faith** – Trusting in the divine support during your transformation.

Reversed: Reversed, The Star indicates a loss of faith or feeling disconnected from your spiritual path. It suggests that doubt, despair, or cynicism is clouding your ability to see the positive outcomes of shadow work. This card encourages you to reconnect with hope and trust in divine timing, even when the path ahead seems unclear.

- **Loss of Faith** – Feeling disconnected from your spiritual path.
- **Confusion** – Struggling to find direction in your healing process.
- **Despair** – Losing hope during challenging phases of shadow work.
- **Lack of Inspiration** – Feeling uninspired to continue your healing journey.
- **Inner Turmoil** – Experiencing emotional chaos that obscures clarity.

The Moon

JACOB'S DREAM AT BETHEL

And Jacob had a dream about a ladder that rested on the earth
with its top reaching up to heaven,
and God's angels were going up and down the ladder.
Genesis 28:12 BSB

Jacob, a key patriarch in the Bible, is known for his complex life full of challenges, transformations, and encounters with the divine. His dream at Bethel is a significant moment of spiritual awakening and promise, where God renews the covenant made with Abraham and Isaac, promising Jacob protection and a multitude of descendants. This story encapsulates the journey from doubt and fear towards faith and understanding, akin to the voyage through the night that The Moon card suggests.

UPRIGHT KEYWORDS:	REVERSED KEYWORDS:
Subconscious	Confusion
Intuition	Fear
Mystery	Deception
Uncertainty	Loss of Direction
Illumination	Illusion

Upright: The Moon represents illusion, the subconscious, and the unknown. In shadow work, this card invites you to explore the hidden depths of your psyche, where your fears and insecurities reside. It symbolizes a period of darkness and uncertainty, where you must confront the shadow parts of yourself that are elusive or difficult to understand. It encourages you to trust your intuition as you navigate this journey.

- **Subconscious** – Exploring the hidden depths of your psyche.
- **Intuition** – Trusting your inner guidance to navigate your shadows.
- **Mystery** – Embracing the unknown aspects of your emotional world.
- **Uncertainty** – Facing the ambiguous and unclear emotions within.
- **Illumination** – Shedding light on hidden fears and insecurities.

Reversed: Reversed, The Moon suggests confusion, deception, or being overwhelmed by the shadow. It warns of being lost in illusion or denial, unable to see the truth clearly. This card asks you to ground yourself in reality and discern between what is real and what is merely a projection of your fears.

- **Confusion** – Struggling to understand your subconscious messages.
- **Fear** – Letting anxiety prevent you from delving deeper.
- **Deception** – Encountering illusions that distort your self-perception.
- **Loss of Direction** – Feeling lost in your emotional exploration.
- **Illusion** – Recognizing and overcoming deceptive self-beliefs.

The Sun

TRIUMPHAL ENTRY INTO JERUSALEM

*The crowds that went ahead of Him and those that followed
were shouting: "Hosanna to the Son of David!"
"Blessed is He who comes in the name of the Lord!"
"Hosanna in the highest!"*
Matthew 21:9 BSB

**19
THE SUN
TRIUMPHAL ENTRY INTO JERUSALEM (MATTHEW 21:1-11)**

The triumphal entry of Jesus into Jerusalem, marks a significant event in Christian tradition, symbolizing Jesus' acknowledgment as king by the people. Riding on a donkey, a humble beast of burden, Jesus entered Jerusalem while crowds spread their cloaks and palm branches on the road, shouting "Hosanna!"—a cry for salvation and a declaration of praise. This moment, fulfilling Old Testament prophecies about the Messiah's arrival, contrasts royal expectations with Jesus' mission of peace and humility. It highlights the dichotomy between worldly power and divine kingship.

UPRIGHT KEYWORDS:	REVERSED KEYWORDS:
Clarity	Diminished Vitality
Joy	Pessimism
Success	False Pride
Enlightenment	Lack of Clarity
Vitality	Setbacks

Upright: The Sun symbolizes clarity, success, and enlightenment. In shadow work, it represents the breakthrough moment when you have integrated your shadow and are now able to live more fully in alignment with your true self. This card reflects the joy, abundance, and fulfillment that come after the hard work of personal transformation. It celebrates the illumination of truth and the restoration of vitality.

- **Clarity** – Achieving a clear understanding of your healed self.

- **Joy** – Experiencing genuine happiness and emotional fulfillment.

- **Success** – Celebrating the achievements of your shadow work.

- **Enlightenment** – Gaining profound insights and self-awareness.

- **Vitality** – Embracing the energy and life that come from healing.

Reversed: In this position, The Sun suggests that there may be obstacles to fully embracing the light within yourself. It may indicate delayed gratification or a struggle to see the positive outcomes of your shadow work. This card encourages you to remain optimistic and trust that the light will eventually break through the clouds of doubt or fear.

- **Diminished Vitality** – Feeling drained despite progress in shadow work.

- **Pessimism** – Struggling to maintain a positive outlook.

- **False Pride** – Letting arrogance overshadow your healing journey.

- **Lack of Clarity** – Experiencing confusion despite efforts to heal.

- **Setbacks** – Facing temporary challenges that disrupt your progress.

Judgment

LAST JUDGMENT

*All the nations will be gathered before Him,
and He will separate the people one from another,
as a shepherd separates the sheep from the goats.*
Matthew 25:32 BSB

The Last Judgment refers to the final and ultimate judgment by God of every individual's deeds in life. It is a moment when the faithful are separated from the unfaithful, leading to either eternal salvation or damnation. This concept emphasizes accountability, the consequences of one's actions, and the possibility of spiritual renewal and redemption.

UPRIGHT KEYWORDS:	REVERSED KEYWORDS:
Rebirth	Resistance to Change
Awakening	Fear of Reckoning
Reflection	Unresolved Issues
Redemption	Stagnation
Transformation	Misjudgment

Upright: Judgment represents rebirth, awakening, and the final reckoning in shadow work. It signifies that you have reached a pivotal moment of clarity and spiritual insight, where the lessons of your shadow are fully understood and integrated. It speaks of renewal, redemption, and a new beginning. It encourages you to reflect on your journey and embrace the new life that awaits you.

- **Rebirth** – Embracing a new phase of your healing journey.
- **Awakening** – Gaining deep self-awareness and understanding.
- **Reflection** – Evaluating your progress and past actions.
- **Redemption** – Forgiving yourself and others to move forward.
- **Transformation** – Undergoing significant personal change and growth.

Reversed: In reverse, Judgment indicates resistance to change or self-doubt about the progress you've made in shadow work. It may suggest a fear of being judged by yourself or others, preventing you from fully stepping into your new identity. This card asks you to trust in the process of renewal and release any lingering doubts or regrets.

- **Resistance to Change** – Avoiding the necessary transformations in shadow work.
- **Fear of Reckoning** – Hesitating to confront your past actions and emotions.
- **Unresolved Issues** – Holding onto guilt or regrets that impede healing.
- **Stagnation** – Feeling stuck and unable to progress in your journey.
- **Misjudgment** – Making flawed decisions that hinder your growth.

The World

NEW JERUSALEM

I saw the holy city, the new Jerusalem,
coming down out of heaven from God,
prepared as a bride adorned for her husband.
Revelation 21:2 BSB

The New Jerusalem is a prophetic vision of a heavenly city, signifying the fulfillment of God's promise of a new, perfect world where God dwells with humanity, and there is no more suffering or death. It represents the culmination of the biblical narrative of redemption, the ultimate reunion of the divine with the mortal, and the achievement of eternal peace and glory.

UPRIGHT KEYWORDS:	REVERSED KEYWORDS:
Completion	Delayed Completion
Fulfillment	Disunity
Harmony	Resistance to Renewal
Unity	Isolation
Achievement	Unrealized Potential

Upright: The World symbolizes completion, fulfillment, and integration. In shadow work, it represents the culmination of your journey, where all aspects of the self—both light and shadow—are fully embraced. Like the New Jerusalem, this card speaks of spiritual wholeness, harmony, and the manifestation of divine purpose. It celebrates the success of your inner work and the alignment of your soul with its highest calling.

- **Completion** – Achieving full integration of your shadow aspects.
- **Fulfillment** – Experiencing a sense of wholeness and satisfaction.
- **Harmony** – Maintaining balance between all parts of yourself.
- **Unity** – Feeling connected with yourself and the divine.
- **Achievement** – Celebrating the successful culmination of your healing journey.

Reversed: This card suggests unfinished business or a delay in reaching full integration. It indicates that there may still be aspects of your shadow that require attention, or that you are resisting closure on certain issues. This card encourages you to tie up loose ends and ensure that you have fully embraced all parts of your journey before moving forward.

- **Delayed Completion** – Feeling unfinished or incomplete in your healing.
- **Disunity** – Struggling to maintain internal harmony.
- **Resistance to Renewal** – Avoiding the final steps of integration.
- **Isolation** – Feeling alone despite achieving milestones.
- **Unrealized Potential** – Failing to fully embrace or recognize your growth.

The Shadow

JACOB WRESTLES WITH GOD

*Then the man said, "Your name will no longer be Jacob,
but Israel, because you have struggled with God and with humans
and have overcome."*

Genesis 32:28

THE SHADOW
JACOB WRESTLES WITH GOD (GENESIS 32:22-32)

On the eve of reuniting with his estranged brother Esau, Jacob spends the night alone. A mysterious figure, later revealed as God, wrestles with him until dawn. Though Jacob's hip is dislocated, he refuses to let go without a blessing. God renames him Israel, meaning "one who struggles with God," signifying his transformation through struggle. This profound encounter symbolizes the human journey of facing inner conflicts, seeking divine connection, and emerging changed. Jacob's wrestling reflects perseverance, humility, and the power of confronting the self to embrace spiritual growth.

UPRIGHT KEYWORDS:	REVERSED KEYWORDS:
Transformation	Avoidance
Revelation	Resistance to Transformation
Integration	Unresolved Conflicts
Spiritual Encounter	Spiritual Stagnation
Growth	Difficulty Accepting Truths

Upright: The Shadow card represents the courageous act of confronting the hidden aspects of the self. It signifies suppressed emotions, fears, and desires rising to the surface, demanding acknowledgment and integration. This card urges self-reflection and honesty, inviting you to embrace your shadows as a source of wisdom and growth. It is a call to explore the root causes of inner conflict, face discomfort with compassion, and transform the shadow into a source of strength.

- **Transformation** – Embracing change through confronting inner conflicts.
- **Revelation** – Uncovering hidden truths about yourself.
- **Integration** – Merging shadow aspects into your conscious self.
- **Spiritual Encounter** – Experiencing a profound connection with the divine.
- **Growth** – Developing through the process of facing your shadows.

Reversed: In the reversed position, The Shadow highlights avoidance, denial, or fear of the unknown parts of the self. It warns against ignoring suppressed emotions or clinging to destructive patterns. This card suggests resistance to change or fear of confronting deeper truths, resulting in stagnation and recurring challenges. However, it also offers an opportunity: by gently engaging with these hidden parts, you can break free from their unconscious grip.

- **Avoidance** – Refusing to confront your hidden truths.
- **Resistance to Transformation** – Rejecting the necessary changes in shadow work.
- **Unresolved Conflicts** – Letting internal battles linger without resolution.
- **Spiritual Stagnation** – Feeling disconnected from your spiritual path.
- **Difficulty Accepting Truths** – Struggling to acknowledge and integrate difficult aspects of yourself.

Chapter 26

The Minor Arcana:

Reflections of Everyday Life

The Minor Arcana in the Biblical Tarot: Shadows of the Soul captures the essence of life's daily struggles, triumphs, and lessons, offering a detailed map of the human experience. Divided into four sacred suits—Candles, Chalices, Feathers, and Grains—these cards represent the interplay of the spiritual, emotional, intellectual, and material realms, echoing the four elements of fire, water, air, and earth.

Each suit tells its own story through biblical narratives, illustrating how our thoughts, emotions, actions, and resources shape our journey. The Minor Arcana grounds the soul's divine path in the tangible experiences of love, ambition, conflict, and growth, providing insight into the choices and challenges of everyday life. These cards remind us that even the most ordinary moments hold the potential for profound transformation, offering wisdom and clarity for those seeking to integrate the light and shadow of their daily existence.

Ace of Candles

MOSES AND THE BURNING BUSH

When the LORD saw that he had gone over to look,
God called out to him from within the bush, "Moses, Moses!"
"Here I am," he answered.
Exodus 3:4 BSB

ACE of CANDLES
MOSES AND THE BURNING BUSH (EXODUS 3)

In the story of Moses and the Burning Bush, Moses encounters God within a miraculously burning bush that is not consumed by the flames. Through this encounter, God calls Moses to lead the Israelites out of Egypt and into freedom, marking the beginning of Moses's spiritual journey and leadership. This moment of divine communication and inspiration is emblematic of the transformative power of faith and purpose.

UPRIGHT KEYWORDS:	REVERSED KEYWORDS:
Revelation	Avoidance
Inspiration	Confusion
Calling	Fear
Potential	Stagnation
Faith	Resistance

Upright: A divine flame sparks within, signaling the start of a profound spiritual awakening or creative endeavor. This card represents revelation, inspiration, and the call to step into your purpose. It encourages bold action and trust in the path ahead, as this moment carries the potential to ignite meaningful transformation and growth.

- **Revelation** – A spark of divine insight illuminates hidden truths.

- **Inspiration** – New ideas or paths emerge from the depths of the soul.

- **Calling** – A pull toward purpose invites deeper exploration.

- **Potential** – The energy to create change begins to stir within.

- **Faith** – Trusting in the process of spiritual awakening.

Reversed: Fear and self-doubt extinguish the flame of inspiration, leaving you hesitant to act on a divine calling. You may feel disconnected from your inner fire, suppressing creative impulses or resisting spiritual growth. This card warns against letting fear block your potential, urging you to confront the doubts holding you back from transformation.

- **Avoidance** – Ignoring a call to confront shadow aspects.

- **Confusion** – Struggling to interpret spiritual or emotional messages.

- **Fear** – Hesitating to embrace transformative insights.

- **Stagnation** – Suppressing creative or spiritual potential.

- **Resistance** – Fighting against inner revelations that challenge comfort zones.

Two of Candles

ELIJAH ON MOUNT CARMEL

Then Elijah approached all the people and said,
"How long will you waver between two opinions?
If the LORD is God, follow Him.
But if Baal is God, follow him."
1 Kings 18:21 BSB

TWO *of* CANDLES
ELIJAH ON MOUNT CARMEL (1 KINGS 18:16-45)

Elijah confronts the prophets of Baal on Mount Carmel to prove to the Israelites that the Lord is the true God. Elijah proposes a test involving two altars: one for Baal and one for the Lord. Despite the prophets of Baal's efforts, their god does not answer by fire. Elijah then prepares his altar, drenches it in water, and prays to the Lord, who responds with fire, consuming the sacrifice. This act leads the people to proclaim the Lord as God. The story highlights Elijah's faith, strategic planning, and the bold execution of his vision amidst uncertainty.

UPRIGHT KEYWORDS:	REVERSED KEYWORDS:
Choice	Doubt
Conviction	Conflict
Challenge	Fear
Clarity	Isolation
Empowerment	Inaction

Upright: You are at a crossroads, called to choose between faith and fear. This card signifies clarity in decision-making, confidence in divine guidance, and the courage to stand firm in your convictions despite opposition. It invites you to align with truth and take decisive action, trusting in God's power to guide you.

- **Choice** – Deciding between faith and fear reveals inner conflict.
- **Conviction** – Standing firm in the face of doubt.
- **Challenge** – Confronting illusions and uncovering truth.
- **Clarity** – Seeing through shadowed perspectives to find resolution.
- **Empowerment** – Choosing to act with courage despite uncertainty.

Reversed: Doubt and indecision cloud your path, creating inner turmoil and hesitation. Fear of making the wrong choice or facing opposition leaves you stuck, unable to move forward. This card warns against avoiding tough decisions and encourages you to confront your fears, trusting that clarity and strength will come through faith.

- **Doubt** – Indecision clouds progress and fosters self-sabotage.
- **Conflict** – Inner turmoil arises from avoiding necessary choices.
- **Fear** – Reluctance to confront deeper truths.
- **Isolation** – Feeling disconnected from guidance or purpose.
- **Inaction** – Stalling growth by ignoring pivotal decisions.

Three of Candles

THE CALL OF ABRAM

Then the LORD said to Abram,
"Leave your country, your kindred, and your father's household,
and go to the land I will show you.
Genesis 12:1 BSB

THREE *of* CANDLES
THE CALL OF ABRAM (GENESIS 12)

God calls Abram (later Abraham) to leave his country, his people, and his father's household for a land that God would show him. In return, God promises to make Abram a great nation, to bless him and make his name great. Abram's obedience to God's call, leaving behind everything he knew for the promise of a greater future, marks the beginning of a significant journey not only for Abram but for the formation of a people through whom God would bless all nations.

UPRIGHT KEYWORDS:	REVERSED KEYWORDS:
Vision	Hesitation
Courage	Short-Sightedness
Exploration	Resistance
Faith	Doubt
Expansion	Stagnation

Upright: A new journey begins, one that requires courage and faith to step into the unknown. This card reflects divine guidance leading you toward growth, expansion, and spiritual transformation. It encourages you to embrace the possibilities ahead with trust, knowing that this path will bring profound blessings and fulfillment.

- **Vision** – A new direction emerges, promising growth and discovery.
- **Courage** – Stepping into the unknown to embrace transformation.
- **Exploration** – Venturing beyond the familiar to uncover hidden truths.
- **Faith** – Trusting the journey, even without clarity on the destination.
- **Expansion** – Shadow work opens the path to spiritual abundance.

Reversed: Resistance to change and fear of uncertainty keep you tethered to the familiar, preventing growth. You may hesitate to answer a divine call, doubting your ability to succeed. This card urges you to confront these fears and trust in the greater vision for your life, as stagnation blocks your transformation.

- **Hesitation** – Fear of leaving comfort zones stifles growth.
- **Short-Sightedness** – Focusing on immediate safety over long-term gain.
- **Resistance** – Denying the need to embark on a transformative journey.
- **Doubt** – Questioning one's ability to navigate uncertainty.
- **Stagnation** – Shadow aspects block movement forward.

Four of Candles

THE ARK BROUGHT TO JERUSALEM

*And David, wearing a linen ephod, danced with all his might
before the LORD, while he and all the house of Israel
brought up the ark of the LORD with shouting
and the sounding of the ram's horn.*
2 Samuel 6:14-16 BSB

FOUR of CANDLES
THE ARK BROUGHT TO JERUSALEM (2 SAMUEL 6)

David successfully brings the Ark of the Covenant to Jerusalem, marking a significant religious and cultural milestone for the Israelites. The Ark's arrival in Jerusalem is met with great celebration, including music, dancing, and offerings. This event not only symbolizes God's presence among the people but also unites them in a collective expression of faith and joy. The story reflects the establishment of Jerusalem as the spiritual center and a collective homecoming for the people of Israel.

UPRIGHT KEYWORDS:	REVERSED KEYWORDS:
Celebration	Disharmony
Unity	Irreverence
Sacredness	Isolation
Reflection	Restlessness
Harmony	Disconnection

Upright: This card signifies celebration, unity, and the fulfillment of spiritual or personal goals. It reflects moments of harmony, gratitude, and reverence for divine blessings. Whether in community or solitude, you are invited to pause and honor the sacred milestones in your journey, basking in the joy and peace they bring.

- **Celebration** – Honoring progress and victories, both inner and outer.
- **Unity** – Embracing connections that bring healing and joy.
- **Sacredness** – Recognizing the holiness in shadow work's challenges.
- **Reflection** – Finding peace in spiritual rituals and moments of gratitude.
- **Harmony** – Reintegrating fragmented parts of the self.

Reversed: Disharmony or neglect disrupts the peace and joy you seek. You may feel disconnected from your spiritual center or fail to appreciate the sacred in your life. This card warns against taking blessings for granted and encourages you to restore balance and gratitude to realign with your sense of purpose.

- **Disharmony** – Struggles in relationships mirror inner conflicts.
- **Irreverence** – Neglecting the importance of sacred reflection.
- **Isolation** – Avoiding communal or spiritual support during shadow work.
- **Restlessness** – Disrupting moments of calm with unresolved fears.
- **Disconnection** – Feeling distant from self or spiritual grounding.

Five of Candles

JOSEPH AND HIS JEALOUS BROTHERS

Come, let us sell him to the Ishmaelites and not lay a hand on him;
for he is our brother, our own flesh."
And they agreed.
Genesis 37:27 BSB

FIVE of CANDLES
JOSEPH AND HIS JEALOUS BROTHERS (GENESIS 37:18-36)

Joseph, the favored son of Jacob, is envied by his brothers because of the special treatment he receives from their father and because of Joseph's dreams that predict his rise to prominence over them. Their jealousy leads them to sell Joseph into slavery. However, this act of betrayal begins Joseph's journey from slave to high-ranking official in Egypt, where he eventually reconciles with his family during a famine. The story encapsulates the complexity of familial relationships, personal growth through adversity, and the ultimate reconciliation and understanding.

UPRIGHT KEYWORDS:	REVERSED KEYWORDS:
Conflict	Resentment
Envy	Betrayal
Growth	Bitterness
Patience	Avoidance
Healing	Isolation

Upright: Conflict and envy arise, reflecting tensions in relationships or inner struggles. This card highlights the need to confront jealousy, resentment, or misunderstanding with patience and wisdom. It points to opportunities for growth through forgiveness and reconciliation, ultimately transforming discord into deeper connection and personal strength.

- **Conflict** – Unresolved emotions surface, demanding attention.
- **Envy** – Recognizing jealousy and its shadow in personal dynamics.
- **Growth** – Overcoming interpersonal struggles to strengthen inner resolve.
- **Patience** – Allowing time for healing and forgiveness.
- **Healing** – Transforming discord into opportunities for reconciliation.

Reversed: Lingering resentment and unresolved conflict weigh heavily on your spirit, creating emotional stagnation. You may struggle with feelings of betrayal or allow bitterness to dominate your interactions. This card encourages you to address these issues directly, letting go of negativity to restore harmony and open the path to healing.

- **Resentment** – Holding grudges prevents emotional release.
- **Betrayal** – Struggling with feelings of trust and betrayal.
- **Bitterness** – Lingering negativity blocks personal growth.
- **Avoidance** – Refusing to address relational wounds.
- **Isolation** – Allowing conflict to create distance rather than resolution.

Six of Candles

THE FALL OF JERICHO

When they heard the blast of the horn,
the people gave a great shout, and the wall collapsed.
Then all the people charged straight into the city and captured it.
Joshua 6:20 BSB

SIX *of* CANDLES
THE FALL OF JERICHO (JOSHUA 6)

In Joshua 6, the Israelites, led by Joshua, conquer the city of Jericho in a miraculous manner. God commands the Israelites to march around the city walls once a day for six days with the priests carrying the Ark of the Covenant and blowing trumpets. On the seventh day, after marching around the city seven times and with a long blast on the trumpets, the Israelites shout, and the walls of Jericho collapse, allowing them to take the city. This story symbolizes the power of divine intervention and the triumph of faith over seemingly insurmountable obstacles.

UPRIGHT KEYWORDS:	REVERSED KEYWORDS:
Breakthrough	Stagnation
Unity	Doubt
Faith	Conflict
Progress	Resistance
Achievement	Delay

Upright: This card symbolizes breakthroughs and victories achieved through faith and persistence. Obstacles crumble when approached with trust in divine timing and guidance. Celebrate the success of your efforts, recognizing the power of unity and perseverance in overcoming even the most insurmountable challenges.

- **Breakthrough** – Obstacles crumble through persistence and faith.
- **Unity** – Collaboration aids in achieving spiritual victories.
- **Faith** – Trusting in divine timing amidst challenges.
- **Progress** – Moving forward with determination and resilience.
- **Achievement** – Celebrating hard-won victories over shadows.

Reversed: Delays and resistance block your progress, leaving you frustrated or stuck before a breakthrough. Doubt in your ability to overcome obstacles may hinder your efforts. This card invites you to realign with your faith and trust the process, as persistence and patience will eventually lead to triumph.

- **Stagnation** – Feeling stuck before breakthroughs occur.
- **Doubt** – Questioning one's ability to overcome obstacles.
- **Conflict** – Lack of alignment hinders success.
- **Resistance** – Avoiding the work needed to break through barriers.
- **Delay** – Spiritual growth slows due to fear or hesitation.

Seven of Candles

DAVID AND GOLIATH

But David said to the Philistine,
"You come against me with sword and spear and javelin,
but I come against you in the name of the LORD of Hosts,
the God of the armies of Israel, whom you have defied.
1 Samuel 17:45 BSB

In the story of David and Goliath (1 Samuel 17), the young shepherd David faces the Philistine giant Goliath, who has been terrorizing the Israelite army. Despite Goliath's formidable size and strength, and the fact that David is armed only with a sling and a few stones, David's faith in God gives him the courage to confront and defeat Goliath. David's victory serves as a profound demonstration of faith, courage, and the power of God working through an individual to overcome seemingly insurmountable odds.

UPRIGHT KEYWORDS:	REVERSED KEYWORDS:
Courage	Fear
Confidence	Weakness
Perseverance	Hesitation
Victory	Defeat
Faith	Isolation

Upright: Courage and determination define this moment, as you face significant challenges with faith and strength. This card reminds you of the power within, urging you to trust in divine support to overcome adversity. Victory comes not through force, but through resilience, confidence, and reliance on higher guidance.

- **Courage** – Facing fears with trust in inner strength.
- **Confidence** – Overcoming challenges through faith.
- **Perseverance** – Standing firm in the face of opposition.
- **Victory** – Triumphing over shadows that seemed insurmountable.
- **Faith** – Leaning on divine support to conquer struggles.

Reversed: Fear and self-doubt overshadow your ability to confront challenges, leaving you feeling weak or overwhelmed. You may hesitate to take necessary action, allowing obstacles to grow larger in your mind. This card urges you to confront your fears and reclaim your inner power to move forward.

- **Fear** – Avoiding challenges due to self-doubt.
- **Weakness** – Allowing insecurities to dictate actions.
- **Hesitation** – Missing opportunities out of fear of failure.
- **Defeat** – Succumbing to shadows without resistance.
- **Isolation** – Feeling alone in the face of adversity.

Eight of Candles

PHILIP AND THE ETHIOPIAN

When they came up out of the water, the Spirit of the Lord carried Philip away, and the eunuch saw him no more, but went on his way rejoicing.
Acts 8:39 BSB

EIGHT *of* CANDLES
PHILIP AND THE ETHIOPIAN (ACTS 8:26-40)

In Acts 8:26-40, Philip, is directed by an angel of the Lord to go south to the road that descends from Jerusalem to Gaza. There, he encounters an Ethiopian eunuch, a high official under the queen of the Ethiopians, reading the Book of Isaiah. Guided by the Spirit, Philip joins the eunuch in his chariot, explains the scriptures to him, and baptizes him. The story illustrates the rapid spread of the Christian message and the immediate response of those who hear and understand it.

UPRIGHT KEYWORDS:	REVERSED KEYWORDS:
Guidance	Missed Opportunities
Connection	Confusion
Awakening	Isolation
Mission	Stagnation
Revelation	Fear

Upright: Guidance and connection define this card, as opportunities arise to share wisdom and offer spiritual insight. It encourages you to embrace divine inspiration and act as both a teacher and student, deepening your understanding of truth while fostering meaningful relationships that inspire growth.

- **Guidance** – Providing clarity to others while exploring your own understanding.
- **Connection** – Building spiritual relationships that enrich growth.
- **Awakening** – Gaining insight into personal and collective shadows.
- **Mission** – Embracing opportunities to share wisdom and truth.
- **Revelation** – Discovering deeper meanings in life's challenges.

Reversed: Missed opportunities for connection or guidance leave you feeling isolated or stuck. Fear of sharing your insights or reluctance to accept help creates stagnation. This card urges you to open yourself to divine wisdom and embrace the connections that can lead to growth and understanding.

- **Missed Opportunities** – Failing to act on moments of divine connection.
- **Confusion** – Difficulty interpreting the messages within shadow work.
- **Isolation** – Avoiding engagement with others or spiritual paths.
- **Stagnation** – Neglecting the call to explore and share insights.
- **Fear** – Doubting your ability to guide or be guided.

Nine of Candles

SATAN TESTS JOB

*In all this, Job did not sin
or charge God with wrongdoing.*
Job 1:22 BSB

NINE *of* CANDLES
SATAN TESTS JOB (JOB 1)

The story of Job (found in the Book of Job) revolves around a righteous man named Job, whose faith is tested by Satan with God's permission. Job suffers tremendous loss, including his wealth, health, and family, yet he refuses to give up on God. Despite the advice of his friends and the urging of his wife, Job maintains his faith, questioning God's reasons but never renouncing his faithfulness. Ultimately, God restores Job's fortunes, doubling what he had before, as a reward for his steadfast faith.

UPRIGHT KEYWORDS:	REVERSED KEYWORDS:
Resilience	Defeat
Endurance	Bitterness
Perseverance	Exhaustion
Wisdom	Doubt
Faith	Resistance

Upright: This card represents resilience and endurance in the face of trials. It encourages you to hold steadfast to your faith and inner strength, even when the challenges feel overwhelming. Through patience and trust, you gain wisdom and insight, transforming hardship into spiritual growth and personal empowerment.

- **Resilience** – Withstanding trials with unwavering faith.
- **Endurance** – Finding strength in the face of prolonged challenges.
- **Perseverance** – Standing firm despite doubt and adversity.
- **Wisdom** – Gaining insight through hardship and introspection.
- **Faith** – Trusting in divine purpose even when shadows loom large.

Reversed: Overwhelmed by struggles, you may feel exhausted or defeated. The weight of adversity drains your spirit, leading to doubt and despair. This card warns against giving in to hopelessness and encourages you to find renewed strength by confronting unresolved fears and embracing perseverance.

- **Defeat** – Feeling overwhelmed by life's trials.
- **Bitterness** – Harboring resentment toward difficulties or perceived injustices.
- **Exhaustion** – Struggling to maintain strength during prolonged challenges.
- **Doubt** – Questioning divine purpose or personal ability.
- **Resistance** – Avoiding lessons hidden within adversity.

Ten of Candles

JEREMIAH'S BURDEN

Why did I come out of the womb to see only trouble and sorrow,
and to end my days in shame?
Jeremiah 20:18 BSB

TEN *of* CANDLES
JEREMIAH'S BURDEN (JEREMIAH 20)

Jeremiah, often called the "weeping prophet," was tasked by God to prophesy the destruction of Judah and Jerusalem due to their unfaithfulness. His messages were met with hostility, rejection, and persecution, making his prophetic mission a heavy burden. Despite the emotional and physical toll, Jeremiah remained committed to his divine calling, enduring great personal suffering to fulfill God's command. His life reflects the struggles of bearing a heavy load for the sake of a higher purpose.

UPRIGHT KEYWORDS:	REVERSED KEYWORDS:
Responsibility	Overwhelm
Dedication	Burnout
Persistence	Avoidance
Clarity	Stagnation
Redemption	Denial

Upright: Carrying a significant responsibility, you feel the weight of truth and purpose pressing heavily upon you. This card reflects the importance of persistence and dedication, even when the path feels overwhelming. It reminds you to trust that your efforts are meaningful and will lead to spiritual fulfillment.

- **Responsibility** – Carrying the weight of truth and accountability.
- **Dedication** – Committing to the spiritual work of transformation.
- **Persistence** – Continuing forward despite the heaviness of the path.
- **Clarity** – Understanding the reasons behind burdens and challenges.
- **Redemption** – Finding meaning and growth in the struggle.

Reversed: The burdens you carry feel unbearable, leaving you stuck in exhaustion or burnout. Avoidance or denial of these responsibilities exacerbates the weight. This card urges you to reassess your load, confront suppressed emotions, and seek support to regain balance and move forward.

- **Overwhelm** – Feeling crushed under the weight of unacknowledged shadows.
- **Burnout** – Neglecting self-care in pursuit of spiritual or personal goals.
- **Avoidance** – Resisting the responsibilities required for growth.
- **Stagnation** – Becoming stuck under unresolved emotional weight.
- **Denial** – Refusing to face or release what burdens you.

Page of Candles

MIRIAM'S PRAISE FOR GOD

And Miriam sang back to them:
"Sing to the LORD, for He is highly exalted;
the horse and rider He has thrown into the sea."
Exodus 15:21 BSB

PAGE *of* CANDLES
MIRIAM'S PRAISE FOR GOD (EXODUS 15:20-21)

After the Israelites successfully crossed the Red Sea and escaped the pursuing Egyptian army, Miriam, the prophetess and sister of Moses and Aaron, led the people in a song and dance of praise to God for their deliverance. This act of worship and celebration, underscores the power of faith and the joy of salvation. Miriam's response to God's miraculous intervention showcases her leadership in worship and her role as a conduit of inspiration and praise among her people.

UPRIGHT KEYWORDS:	REVERSED KEYWORDS:
Inspiration	Immaturity
Joy	Frustration
Creativity	Negativity
Curiosity	Impatience
Faith	Resistance

Upright: This card symbolizes joy, inspiration, and a fresh perspective in your spiritual journey. It invites you to approach challenges with curiosity and creativity, celebrating moments of growth and discovery. Trust in divine guidance as you take your first steps toward deeper understanding and expression.

- **Inspiration** – Celebrating small victories and moments of growth.
- **Joy** – Embracing the light within shadow work.
- **Creativity** – Using imaginative energy to explore inner truths.
- **Curiosity** – Approaching challenges with a fresh and open perspective.
- **Faith** – Trusting in divine guidance during the journey.

Reversed: Struggling to find joy or inspiration, you may feel frustrated or impatient with the process of growth. Immaturity or distraction keeps you from focusing on meaningful progress. This card reminds you to reconnect with your purpose and approach shadow work with an open and willing heart.

- **Immaturity** – Avoiding responsibilities in favor of distractions.
- **Frustration** – Struggling to find joy in the process of growth.
- **Negativity** – Allowing doubt to overshadow moments of progress.
- **Impatience** – Rushing through shadow work without reflection.
- **Resistance** – Avoiding spiritual growth through fear of vulnerability.

Knight of Candles

JOSHUA - LEADER OF FAITH

Have I not commanded you to be strong and courageous?
Do not be afraid; do not be discouraged,
for the LORD your God is with you wherever you go."
Joshua 1:9 BSB

Joshua, the successor to Moses, was charged with leading the Israelites into Canaan, the Promised Land. Under his leadership, the Israelites experienced miraculous victories, including the fall of Jericho, showcasing Joshua's unwavering faith in God's promises. His story, notably his courage to act upon God's commands and his role in fulfilling the divine plan, highlights the qualities of leadership, faith, and the willingness to embark on a challenging journey despite the obstacles.

UPRIGHT KEYWORDS:	REVERSED KEYWORDS:
Determination	Recklessness
Courage	Stagnation
Leadership	Self-Doubt
Purpose	Arrogance
Faithfulness	Fear

Upright: This card represents bold action and unwavering determination. You are called to lead with courage and confidence, trusting in divine guidance as you confront challenges and pursue your purpose. It encourages disciplined effort and faith in the face of uncertainty, reminding you of your strength and resolve.

- **Determination** – Taking bold steps toward growth and understanding.
- **Courage** – Facing personal challenges with unwavering resolve.
- **Leadership** – Inspiring others through example and perseverance.
- **Purpose** – Moving forward with clear direction and intent.
- **Faithfulness** – Trusting in divine plans during uncertainty.

Reversed: Reckless behavior or fear of failure may disrupt your progress, leaving you stagnant or unsure of your direction. Arrogance or impatience can blind you to the lessons within shadow work. This card urges you to slow down, reflect, and realign with your inner purpose.

- **Recklessness** – Acting impulsively without reflection.
- **Stagnation** – Losing momentum in the face of challenges.
- **Self-Doubt** – Questioning your ability to lead or grow.
- **Arrogance** – Overlooking the lessons of humility within shadow work.
- **Fear** – Avoiding bold action due to insecurity.

Queen of Candles

DEBORAH - PROPHETESS AND LEADER

Now Deborah, a prophetess, the wife of Lappidoth,
was judging Israel at that time.
Judges 4:4 BSB

QUEEN *of* CANDLES
DEBORAH (PROPHETESS AND LEADER (JUDGES 4)

Deborah, one of the major judges of Israel, was a prophetess and the only female judge mentioned in the Bible. She led Israel at a time of oppression and commanded Barak to lead an army against the Canaanite king Jabin and his military commander Sisera. Deborah's leadership and faith in God's command led to a significant victory for Israel. Her story is celebrated in the "Song of Deborah," a victory hymn that praises God for the triumph over the Canaanites, showcasing her wisdom, courage, and effective leadership.

UPRIGHT KEYWORDS:	REVERSED KEYWORDS:
Wisdom	Control
Authority	Doubt
Inspiration	Isolation
Strength	Fear
Vision	Rigidity

Upright: This card embodies wisdom, authority, and compassionate leadership. You are called to inspire others with your insight and vision, guiding them toward clarity and growth. It encourages you to lead with grace and strength, balancing determination with empathy as you navigate challenges.

- **Wisdom** – Offering insight gained from personal and spiritual experience.
- **Authority** – Leading with confidence and compassion.
- **Inspiration** – Encouraging others to face their shadows with courage.
- **Strength** – Balancing grace and determination in difficult times.
- **Vision** – Seeing the bigger picture and guiding others toward clarity.

Reversed: Doubt or fear of responsibility may prevent you from stepping into your full potential as a leader. Overpowering others or resisting the lessons of shadow work can create imbalance. This card invites you to reconnect with your inner wisdom and lead with humility and purpose.

- **Control** – Overpowering others instead of guiding them.
- **Doubt** – Questioning your own wisdom and decisions.
- **Isolation** – Withdrawing from the responsibility of leadership.
- **Fear** – Avoiding necessary confrontation within shadow work.
- **Rigidity** – Refusing to adapt to the lessons shadow work presents.

King of Candles

KING DAVID

I have been with you wherever you have gone,
and I have cut off all your enemies from before you.
Now I will make for you a name
like that of the greatest in the land.
2 Samuel 7:9 BSB

David's rise from shepherd boy to the King of Israel is a story of divine favor, personal bravery, and strategic brilliance. David gains fame by defeating Goliath, earns the love of the people, and navigates the complex political landscape of his time with astuteness. His reign is marked by military conquests and cultural achievements - his poetic psalms. However, David's life is also fraught with personal failings, including his affair with Bathsheba and the resultant turmoil within his own family, illustrating the dual nature of his legacy as both a revered leader and a flawed man.

UPRIGHT KEYWORDS:	REVERSED KEYWORDS:
Leadership	Arrogance
Strength	Corruption
Wisdom	Weakness
Creativity	Regret
Legacy	Stubbornness

Upright: As a symbol of wisdom, strength, and creative leadership, this card calls you to guide others with integrity and faith. It reflects the balance between power and humility, urging you to make decisions grounded in spiritual growth and personal insight. Inspire others by embracing your role as a compassionate and visionary leader.

- **Leadership** – Guiding others with integrity and faith.
- **Strength** – Balancing power with humility.
- **Wisdom** – Making decisions informed by spiritual and personal growth.
- **Creativity** – Using imagination and passion to overcome challenges.
- **Legacy** – Building a foundation of trust and inspiration for others.

Reversed: Misuse of power or unresolved shadows may cloud your judgment, leading to arrogance or self-doubt. Past mistakes or fear of failure can hinder your ability to lead effectively. This card urges you to confront these challenges, integrate lessons from shadow work, and lead with renewed purpose and grace.

- **Arrogance** – Allowing pride to overshadow growth.
- **Corruption** – Misusing power or influence in shadowed ways.
- **Weakness** – Failing to confront personal or spiritual struggles.
- **Regret** – Focusing on past mistakes instead of moving forward.
- **Stubbornness** – Refusing to embrace change or accept guidance.

Ace of Chalices

SAMARITAN WOMAN AT THE WELL

*..But whoever drinks the water I give him will never thirst.
Indeed, the water I give him will become in him
a fount of water springing up to eternal life."*
John 4:14 BSB

ACE of CHALICES
SAMARITAN WOMAN AT THE WELL (JOHN 4)

Jesus, traveling through Samaria, stops at Jacob's well, where He encounters a Samaritan woman. In the course of their conversation, Jesus reveals knowledge, which astonishes her, and speaks of offering "living water" that would forever quench her thirst. This encounter transforms the woman, who goes on to share her experience with others in her community, leading many to believe in Jesus. The story is a powerful depiction of Jesus's compassion, the breaking of social barriers, and the offer of spiritual awakening and redemption.

UPRIGHT KEYWORDS:	REVERSED KEYWORDS:
Renewal	Blocked Emotions
Love	Disconnection
Intuition	Emotional Depletion
Abundance	Avoidance
Healing	Resistance

Upright: This card represents an outpouring of spiritual and emotional renewal. Like the Samaritan woman at the well, you are offered divine grace and a chance for deep healing. It signifies new beginnings in love, emotional growth, and spiritual awakening, inviting you to open your heart to divine connection and fulfillment.

- **Renewal** – A fresh emotional or spiritual awakening offers healing and growth.

- **Love** – Open yourself to receiving and sharing unconditional love.

- **Intuition** – Deep emotional truths flow into your awareness.

- **Abundance** – Embrace the fullness of life as divine grace overflows.

- **Healing** – Old wounds begin to mend, creating space for wholeness.

Reversed: Emotional barriers block the flow of grace and connection. You may feel disconnected from yourself or others, avoiding the healing opportunities before you. This card warns against ignoring emotional needs or rejecting divine guidance, urging you to address inner resistance and reconnect with your true self.

- **Blocked Emotions** – Suppressed feelings prevent healing and connection.

- **Disconnection** – A sense of detachment from self or others hinders progress.

- **Emotional Depletion** – Neglecting self-care drains your inner resources.

- **Avoidance** – Fears around vulnerability keep you from embracing growth.

- **Resistance** – Refusing to address emotional pain delays transformation.

Two of Chalices

THE BOND OF DAVID AND JONATHAN

*Then Jonathan made a covenant with David
because he loved him as himself.*
1 Samuel 18:3 BSB

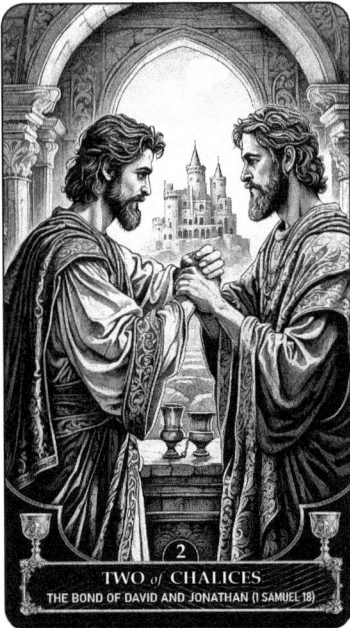

TWO *of* CHALICES
THE BOND OF DAVID AND JONATHAN (1 SAMUEL 18)

The friendship between David and Jonathan is one of the most significant relationships in the Bible, depicted in the Books of 1 Samuel. Jonathan, the son of King Saul, and David, who would become Israel's greatest king, formed an immediate and strong bond. Despite Saul's jealousy of David and his attempts to kill him, Jonathan's loyalty to David never wavered. Their story is a testament to loyalty, sacrifice, and an unbreakable emotional bond that transcends familial ties and political intrigue.

UPRIGHT KEYWORDS:	REVERSED KEYWORDS:
Partnership	Disharmony
Connection	Betrayal
Unity	Imbalance
Healing	Conflict
Balance	Isolation

Upright: This card symbolizes deep, mutual connection and trust, as seen in the bond between David and Jonathan. It reflects harmony, partnership, and shared purpose, whether in love, friendship, or collaboration. A powerful union rooted in loyalty and mutual respect brings emotional balance and joy.

- **Partnership** – Balanced, mutual relationships bring harmony and support.
- **Connection** – Deep emotional bonds foster trust and growth.
- **Unity** – Collaboration aligns with shared goals and values.
- **Healing** – Strengthening emotional ties helps mend past wounds.
- **Balance** – A healthy give-and-take ensures stability in relationships.

Reversed: Disharmony and mistrust disrupt the potential for meaningful connection. Miscommunication or unresolved conflict may create distance in relationships. This card encourages you to address emotional imbalances and seek reconciliation to rebuild trust and restore harmony.

- **Disharmony** – Misalignment creates tension and distance in relationships.
- **Betrayal** – Breaches of trust cause emotional pain and withdrawal.
- **Imbalance** – Unequal effort disrupts the flow of connection.
- **Conflict** – Unresolved issues threaten the stability of bonds.
- **Isolation** – Fear of vulnerability prevents meaningful connections.

Three of Chalices

THE WEDDING AT CANA

...and the master of the banquet tasted the water that had been turned into wine. He did not know where it was from, but the servants who had drawn the water knew.
John 2:9 BSB

THREE *of* CHALICES
THE WEDDING AT CANA (JOHN 2:1-11)

At the Wedding at Cana, Jesus, His mother Mary, and His disciples are guests. When the wine runs out, Mary tells Jesus, prompting Him to perform a miracle. Jesus instructs the servants to fill jars with water, which He then turns into wine, not only solving the problem but providing wine of superior quality. This act not only saves the hosts from social embarrassment but also reveals Jesus's divine power to His disciples, deepening their faith. The story is celebrated as a sign of Jesus's glory and His ability to transform the mundane into the extraordinary.

UPRIGHT KEYWORDS:	REVERSED KEYWORDS:
Celebration	Superficiality
Community	Disconnection
Abundance	Overindulgence
Support	Neglect
Harmony	Conflict

Upright: A time of celebration, joy, and community comes to light. Like the wedding at Cana, this card reflects shared happiness, emotional fulfillment, and gratitude. It invites you to embrace life's blessings and cherish the bonds that bring you together with others in harmony and love.

- **Celebration** – Rejoice in shared achievements and emotional fulfillment.
- **Community** – Connection with others fosters joy and gratitude.
- **Abundance** – Appreciate life's blessings with an open heart.
- **Support** – Strengthen bonds through collaboration and shared joy.
- **Harmony** – Align your emotional energy with those who uplift you.

Reversed: Neglecting joy or taking relationships for granted may create disconnection or imbalance. Overindulgence or shallow connections might overshadow meaningful relationships. This card encourages you to reassess your priorities and nurture authentic bonds to restore emotional fulfillment and harmony.

- **Superficiality** – Shallow connections hinder deeper emotional growth.
- **Disconnection** – Neglecting relationships leads to isolation.
- **Overindulgence** – Excessive focus on pleasure disrupts balance.
- **Neglect** – Failing to nurture bonds creates distance and strain.
- **Conflict** – Tensions within the group diminish harmony.

Four of Chalices

JONAH'S ANGER

And now, O LORD, please take my life from me,
for it is better for me to die than to live."
Jonah 4:3 BSB

FOUR *of* CHALICES
JONAH'S ANGER (JONAH 4)

After Jonah finally obeys God's command to warn Nineveh of impending destruction, the city repents, and God spares it. Rather than rejoicing in the mercy shown, Jonah becomes angry and frustrated with God's compassion towards the Ninevites. He retreats outside the city, hoping to witness its destruction, and laments his own discomfort under a withering plant that had provided him shade. God then questions Jonah's anger, and points out Jonah's lack of compassion for the people of Nineveh. The story illustrates Jonah's struggle with accepting God's will and the lesson of divine mercy and compassion.

UPRIGHT KEYWORDS:	REVERSED KEYWORDS:
Apathy	Discontent
Reflection	Avoidance
Dissatisfaction	Isolation
Stagnation	Negativity
Missed Opportunities	Awakening

Upright: This card represents dissatisfaction and introspection, reflecting Jonah's struggle with anger and frustration. It urges you to reassess your emotional state and consider whether your focus on perceived losses blinds you to divine gifts and opportunities for growth.

- **Apathy** – Emotional detachment signals a need for introspection.
- **Reflection** – Consider what truly fulfills you beyond surface-level desires.
- **Dissatisfaction** – Discontent pushes you to reevaluate your choices.
- **Stagnation** – Feeling stuck invites the opportunity for deeper self-exploration.
- **Missed Opportunities** – Focusing on perceived lacks blinds you to blessings.

Reversed: Disengagement or apathy may prevent you from moving forward. Resistance to accepting divine grace or lessons keeps you stuck in negative patterns. This card encourages you to confront inner dissatisfaction and embrace the opportunity for renewal.

- **Discontent** – Resisting change perpetuates emotional frustration.
- **Avoidance** – Fear of confronting emotions delays growth.
- **Isolation** – Withdrawal from connections deepens feelings of dissatisfaction.
- **Negativity** – Focusing solely on what's wrong prevents progress.
- **Awakening** – Ignoring inner calls for renewal stalls your evolution.

Five of Chalices

THE PRODIGAL SON

After he had spent all he had,
a severe famine swept through that country,
and he began to be in need.
Luke 15:14 BSB

The parable of the Prodigal Son tells of a young man who asks for his inheritance early, then squanders his wealth in a foreign land, leading to destitution. Upon hitting rock bottom, he decides to return to his father, expecting to be treated as a servant. To his surprise, his father welcomes him with open arms, celebrating his return as if he were dead and is now alive again. The older brother, who stayed and worked diligently, resents the celebration for the wayward son, highlighting themes of jealousy and the challenge of unconditional love and forgiveness.

UPRIGHT KEYWORDS:	REVERSED KEYWORDS:
Loss	Regret
Forgiveness	Bitterness
Reflection	Resistance
Redemption	Isolation
Healing	Stagnation

Upright: This card reflects sorrow, regret, and the need for forgiveness. Like the prodigal son, it reminds you that reconciliation and healing are always possible. Though you may feel loss, hope and redemption await if you focus on what remains and move toward emotional restoration.

- **Loss** – Grieve what's been lost while recognizing the potential for healing.
- **Forgiveness** – Releasing guilt or resentment brings emotional freedom.
- **Reflection** – Learn from past mistakes to foster growth.
- **Redemption** – Accept grace and move toward reconciliation.
- **Healing** – Transform pain into wisdom through forgiveness and understanding.

Reversed: Dwelling on past mistakes or refusing to forgive yourself or others creates stagnation. Emotional isolation and bitterness block the healing process. This card encourages you to release resentment and embrace the grace of forgiveness and renewal.

- **Regret** – Dwelling on the past prevents emotional recovery.
- **Bitterness** – Holding onto resentment stifles healing and growth.
- **Resistance** – Refusing to forgive keeps wounds open.
- **Isolation** – Emotional withdrawal perpetuates feelings of loss.
- **Stagnation** – Focusing on pain delays opportunities for redemption.

Six of Chalices

JESUS AND THE CHILDREN

But when Jesus saw this, He was indignant and told them,
"Let the little children come to Me, and do not hinder them!
For the kingdom of God belongs to such as these.
Mark 10:14 BSB

SIX of CHALICES
JESUS AND THE CHILDREN (MARK 10:13-16)

In Mark 10:13-16, people bring children to Jesus, but the disciples rebuke them. Jesus, displeased, tells the disciples to let the children come to Him and not to hinder them, for the kingdom of God belongs to such as these. He then blesses the children. This moment underscores the value Jesus places on the qualities of children, such as innocence and trust, as essential for entering the kingdom of God.

UPRIGHT KEYWORDS:	REVERSED KEYWORDS:
Innocence	Clinging to the Past
Nostalgia	Immaturity
Generosity	Regret
Harmony	Stagnation
Connection	Detachment

Upright: This card reflects innocence, joy, and the simplicity of unconditional love. Like Jesus welcoming the children, it invites you to reconnect with childlike wonder and emotional purity. Cherish the moments that bring joy and strengthen bonds of love and kindness.

- **Innocence** – Reconnect with childlike joy and emotional purity.
- **Nostalgia** – Reflect on positive memories to inspire healing.
- **Generosity** – Acts of kindness bring emotional fulfillment.
- **Harmony** – Rediscover balance through simple joys.
- **Connection** – Strengthen bonds with loved ones through care and compassion.

Reversed: Clinging to the past or overidealizing it may hinder growth. Immature emotional patterns or fear of moving forward prevent progress. This card encourages you to release nostalgia and embrace the present with gratitude and clarity.

- **Clinging to the Past** – Overidealizing memories hinders present growth.
- **Immaturity** – Avoidance of responsibilities disrupts progress.
- **Regret** – Unresolved past issues weigh on your emotional state.
- **Stagnation** – Refusal to let go of old patterns blocks evolution.
- **Detachment** – Disconnection from the present diminishes fulfillment.

Seven of Chalices

THE TEMPTATION OF CHRIST

He said to him, "I will give you all of these things,
if you will fall down and worship me."
Matthew 4:9 WEB

SEVEN *of* CHALICES
THE TEMPTATION OF CHRIST (MATTHEW 4:1-11)

After fasting for 40 days and nights in the wilderness, Jesus is tempted by the devil. First, Satan tempts Him to turn stones into bread, challenging His hunger. Next, he challenges Jesus to throw Himself down from the pinnacle of the temple in Jerusalem, questioning God's protection. Finally, Satan offers all the kingdoms of the world in exchange for worship. Jesus rebuffs each temptation with scripture, emphasizing reliance on God and adherence to spiritual truth over earthly power or physical needs.

UPRIGHT KEYWORDS:	REVERSED KEYWORDS:
Choices	Confusion
Temptation	Distraction
Vision	Disillusionment
Illusion	Avoidance
Introspection	Self-Deception

Upright: This card represents choices, illusions, and the challenge of discernment. Like the temptation of Christ, it reflects the struggle to choose wisely when faced with desires or distractions. Focus on what aligns with your higher purpose to avoid being led astray.

- **Choices** – Multiple options require discernment to avoid illusion.
- **Temptation** – Evaluate desires carefully to stay aligned with your purpose.
- **Vision** – Dreams and possibilities emerge, offering inspiration.
- **Illusion** – Beware of being misled by appearances.
- **Introspection** – Shadow work reveals hidden motivations behind choices.

Reversed: Confusion and indecision cloud your ability to choose. Illusions or fear of making the wrong decision create stagnation. This card urges you to ground yourself in truth and confront the shadows influencing your perceptions.

- **Confusion** – Lack of clarity creates indecision and frustration.
- **Distraction** – Overwhelmed by options, you lose focus on priorities.
- **Disillusionment** – Unrealistic expectations lead to disappointment.
- **Avoidance** – Fear of commitment prevents progress.
- **Self-Deception** – Ignoring truths about desires prolongs stagnation.

Eight of Chalices

THE ASCENSION OF JESUS

After He had said this, they watched as He was taken up,
and a cloud hid Him from their sight.
Acts 1:9 BSB

EIGHT of CHALICES
THE ASCENSION OF JESUS (ACTS 1:6-11)

After His resurrection, Jesus appears to His disciples, teaching them about the kingdom of God. At the Mount of Olives, as He blesses them, He is taken up into heaven in their sight, ascending to His Father and signaling the end of His earthly ministry. The disciples are then told by two angels that Jesus will return in the same way He was taken up. This moment of ascension marks a pivotal point for the disciples, urging them to embrace their mission with faith and courage, despite the physical absence of Jesus.

UPRIGHT KEYWORDS:	REVERSED KEYWORDS:
Departure	Fear of Letting Go
Transformation	Stagnation
Spiritual Growth	Uncertainty
Release	Avoidance
Courage	Attachment

Upright: This card reflects leaving behind what no longer serves you and moving toward spiritual fulfillment. Like the ascension of Jesus, it represents the end of one chapter and the beginning of a higher purpose. Embrace the journey of growth and self-discovery.

- **Departure** – Leaving behind what no longer serves your growth.
- **Transformation** – Embracing change as a gateway to deeper fulfillment.
- **Spiritual Growth** – Moving toward a higher purpose and alignment.
- **Release** – Letting go of attachments to find clarity and peace.
- **Courage** – Facing the unknown with faith and determination.

Reversed: Fear of letting go or reluctance to move on keeps you trapped in emotional stagnation. Clinging to the past prevents spiritual progression. This card urges you to confront your fears and trust in the divine plan for renewal.

- **Fear of Letting Go** – Clinging to the past prevents growth.
- **Stagnation** – Resistance to change keeps you trapped in emotional cycles.
- **Uncertainty** – Doubts about your path create hesitation.
- **Avoidance** – Refusing to confront what needs to be released.
- **Attachment** – Holding onto what's familiar blocks spiritual progress.

Nine of Chalices

THE FEAST OF PURIM

*...as the days on which the Jews gained rest from their enemies
and the month in which their sorrow turned to joy and their
mourning into a holiday. He wrote that these were to be days
of feasting and joy, of sending gifts to one another and to the poor.*
Esther 9:22 BSB

NINE *of* CHALICES
THE FEAST OF PURIM (ESTHER 9:20-32)

The story centers around Esther, a Jewish queen of Persia, and her cousin Mordecai, who uncover a plot by Haman, the king's advisor, to annihilate the Jewish people. Through courage, strategic planning, and Esther's intervention with the king, Haman's plans are thwarted. Haman is executed, and the king grants the Jews the right to defend themselves against their enemies. The victory is so complete that it initiates the annual celebration of Purim, marked by feasting, joy, and the exchange of gifts, as a memorial to their deliverance.

UPRIGHT KEYWORDS:	REVERSED KEYWORDS:
Fulfillment	Overindulgence
Joy	Discontent
Gratitude	Imbalance
Contentment	Neglect
Abundance	Shallowness

Upright: This card signifies emotional and material satisfaction, reflecting the joy and gratitude of the Feast of Purim. It encourages you to celebrate your achievements, acknowledge your blessings, and embrace the abundance that comes from aligning with your higher purpose.

- **Fulfillment** – Emotional and material satisfaction brings a sense of completion.
- **Joy** – Celebrate your achievements and the blessings in your life.
- **Gratitude** – Appreciate the abundance that surrounds you.
- **Contentment** – Peace comes from aligning with your inner values.
- **Abundance** – Revel in the emotional and spiritual richness you've cultivated.

Reversed: Overindulgence or misplaced priorities may create discontent. A focus on superficial gains leaves deeper emotional needs unmet. This card encourages you to reassess your values and seek fulfillment that resonates with your spirit.

- **Overindulgence** – Excessive focus on pleasures leaves deeper needs unmet.
- **Discontent** – Surface-level satisfaction masks emotional emptiness.
- **Imbalance** – Over-prioritizing material gains disrupts emotional harmony.
- **Neglect** – Failing to appreciate blessings creates dissatisfaction.
- **Shallowness** – Avoiding deeper connections or reflections hinders growth.

Ten of Chalices

ELIZABETH AND ZECHARIAH'S JOY

He will be a joy and delight to you,
and many will rejoice at his birth,
Luke 1:14 BSB

TEN *of* CHALICES
ELIZABETH AND ZECHARIAH'S JOY (LUKE 1:14-17)

Elizabeth and Zechariah, though righteous and blameless before God, were without children because Elizabeth was barren. Zechariah, a priest, encounters an angel while serving in the temple, who tells him they will have a son named John, who will be great before the Lord. Zechariah doubts the angel, and he is rendered mute until the prophecy is fulfilled. Elizabeth conceives, recognizing the child as a blessing from God. Upon John's birth and Zechariah's affirmation of his name, Zechariah's speech is restored, and they are filled with joy and the Holy Spirit, praising God for His mercy and fulfillment of His promises.

UPRIGHT KEYWORDS:	REVERSED KEYWORDS:
Harmony	Disharmony
Family	Disconnection
Gratitude	Disillusionment
Contentment	Neglect
Wholeness	Imbalance

Upright: This card represents emotional harmony and spiritual fulfillment, reflecting the joy of Elizabeth and Zechariah. It signifies deep connections, family unity, and the realization of long-awaited blessings. Embrace this moment of profound gratitude and love.

- **Harmony** – Emotional fulfillment and spiritual peace flourish in your relationships.
- **Family** – Strong bonds bring lasting joy and unity. **Gratitude** – Celebrate the blessings and achievements you've cultivated.
- **Contentment** – A sense of completion brings balance to your emotional and spiritual life.
- **Wholeness** – Embrace the joy of living in alignment with your purpose.

Reversed: Emotional disharmony or unmet expectations may disrupt peace and happiness. Misalignment in relationships or neglect of spiritual connections creates distance. This card urges you to address imbalances and restore harmony with love and patience.

- **Disharmony** – Conflicts or unmet expectations disrupt emotional peace.
- **Disconnection** – Struggles in relationships create distance and strain.
- **Disillusionment** – Unrealistic ideals about happiness lead to frustration.
- **Neglect** – Failing to nurture relationships erodes emotional bonds.
- **Imbalance** – Inner dissatisfaction disrupts the harmony you seek.

Page of Chalices

SAMUEL, THE BOY PROPHET

Then the LORD came and stood there, calling as before,
"Samuel! Samuel!" And Samuel answered,
"Speak, for Your servant is listening."
1 Samuel 3:10 BSB

PAGE of CHALICES
SAMUEL, THE BOY PROPHET (1 SAMUEL 3)

The story of Samuel begins with his mother, Hannah, praying for a child and promising to dedicate him to God's service. Samuel is born and, true to her word, Hannah brings him to serve under Eli, the priest, at the temple. One night, God calls to Samuel, and with Eli's guidance, Samuel responds, "Speak, for your servant is listening." This marks the beginning of Samuel's journey as a prophet, chosen by God to deliver messages to Israel. Samuel grows up to be a respected prophet, known for his integrity and his role in anointing the first two kings of Israel, Saul and David.

UPRIGHT KEYWORDS:	REVERSED KEYWORDS:
Curiosity	Immaturity
Creativity	Insecurity
Intuition	Stagnation
Innocence	Self-Doubt
Potential	Disconnection

Upright: This card symbolizes curiosity, emotional growth, and spiritual insight. Like Samuel hearing God's call, it invites you to approach life with an open heart and embrace new emotional and spiritual discoveries. Be ready to learn and grow.

- **Curiosity** – Embrace new emotional and spiritual experiences with an open heart.
- **Creativity** – Explore imaginative ways to understand and express your feelings.
- **Intuition** – Pay attention to inner guidance as you navigate emotional growth.
- **Innocence** – Approach challenges with the wisdom of humility and curiosity.
- **Potential** – A fresh perspective opens the door to new possibilities.

Reversed: Emotional immaturity or resistance to growth blocks your path. Fear of vulnerability or rejection may prevent meaningful connections. This card encourages you to confront these fears and open yourself to the lessons of shadow work.

- **Immaturity** – Avoidance of responsibilities delays growth.
- **Insecurity** – Fear of rejection or failure hinders emotional progress.
- **Stagnation** – Resistance to exploring feelings keeps you stuck.
- **Self-Doubt** – Lack of confidence blocks your creative potential.
- **Disconnection** – Ignoring intuition or emotional cues creates imbalance.

Knight of Chalices

YOUNG DAVID

And whenever the spirit from God came upon Saul, David would pick up his harp and play. Then Saul would find relief and feel better, and the spirit of distress would depart from him.
1 Samuel 16:23 BSB

KNIGHT *of* CHALICES
YOUNG DAVID (1 SAMUEL 16:14–23)

When David is brought to Saul's court for the first time. Saul is tormented by an evil spirit, and it is suggested that a skilled harpist might soothe him. David, known both for his bravery and his musical talent, is summoned to play the lyre for Saul. David's music successfully calms Saul, driving the evil spirit away and bringing peace to the troubled king. This episode showcases David's gentle, compassionate side and his ability to bring healing and comfort through his artistry and presence.

UPRIGHT KEYWORDS:	REVERSED KEYWORDS:
Passion	Impulsiveness
Romanticism	Disillusionment
Faith	Overidealism
Determination	Inconsistency
Vision	Avoidance

Upright: This card represents the pursuit of emotional and spiritual ideals with courage and passion. Like young David, it reflects a heart full of faith and a willingness to act on divine inspiration. Trust in your ability to follow your dreams with conviction.

- **Passion** – Pursue emotional and spiritual ideals with courage and heart.
- **Romanticism** – Embrace the beauty and depth of life's emotional experiences.
- **Faith** – Trust in your purpose as you follow your dreams.
- **Determination** – Stay true to your path, even when challenges arise.
- **Vision** – Let your imagination guide you toward deeper understanding.

Reversed: Overidealism or impulsiveness may lead to disappointment. Emotional naivety or unrealistic expectations create instability. This card urges you to temper your enthusiasm with discernment and reflect on your motivations.

- **Impulsiveness** – Acting on emotions without reflection leads to instability.
- **Disillusionment** – Unrealistic expectations create disappointment.
- **Overidealism** – Focusing on fantasy rather than reality hinders growth.
- **Inconsistency** – Difficulty committing to emotional or spiritual goals.
- **Avoidance** – Escaping challenges instead of addressing them delays progress.

Queen of Chalices

HANNAH - MOTHER OF FAITH

I prayed for this boy, and since the LORD has granted me what I asked of Him, I now dedicate the boy to the LORD. For as long as he lives, he is dedicated to the LORD."
1 Samuel 1:27-28 BSB

QUEEN *of* CHALICES
HANNAH - MOTHER OF FAITH (1 SAMUEL 1)

Hannah, deeply distressed by her inability to bear children, prays fervently to God at the temple in Shiloh, promising that if He gives her a son, she will dedicate him to the Lord's service. Eli, the priest, initially mistakes her silent prayers for drunkenness, but upon understanding her sincerity, blesses her wish. God hears Hannah's prayers, and she conceives Samuel, whom she later brings to the temple to serve God, fulfilling her vow. Hannah's story is a poignant testament to faith, perseverance, and the profound bond between mother and child.

UPRIGHT KEYWORDS:	REVERSED KEYWORDS:
Compassion	Overextension
Intuition	Imbalance
Nurturing	Suppressed Emotions
Resilience	Insecurity
Empathy	Isolation

Upright: This card embodies nurturing, intuition, and emotional depth. Like Hannah, it reflects the strength found in faith and the wisdom of listening to your heart. It encourages you to support others with compassion while honoring your own emotional needs.

- **Compassion** – Offer love and support to yourself and others with grace.
- **Intuition** – Trust your inner wisdom to guide emotional decisions.
- **Nurturing** – Cultivate emotional and spiritual connections with care.
- **Resilience** – Strengthen yourself through faith and emotional understanding.
- **Empathy** – Understand others' feelings to foster deeper bonds.

Reversed: Emotional exhaustion or neglect of self-care leaves you feeling drained. Overextending yourself or ignoring intuition creates imbalance. This card urges you to set healthy boundaries and reconnect with your inner strength.

- **Overextension** – Neglecting self-care drains your emotional reserves.
- **Imbalance** – Overgiving disrupts personal boundaries and well-being.
- **Suppressed Emotions** – Ignoring your feelings creates inner tension.
- **Insecurity** – Doubt in your abilities weakens your emotional strength.
- **Isolation** – Emotional withdrawal prevents connection and healing.

King of Chalices

NEHEMIAH REBUILDING JERUSALEM

"You see the trouble we are in. Jerusalem lies in ruins, and its gates have been burned down. Come, let us rebuild the wall of Jerusalem, so that we will no longer be a disgrace."
Nehemiah 2:17 BSB

KING *of* CHALICES
NEHEMIAH REBUILDING JERUSALEM (NEHEMIAH 2:17–18)

Nehemiah, serving as the cupbearer to the Persian king Artaxerxes, learns of the desolation of Jerusalem and its walls. Moved by this news, he prays to God and seeks the king's permission to rebuild Jerusalem. Granted authority and resources, Nehemiah travels to Jerusalem and organizes the reconstruction efforts, overcoming obstacles such as local opposition and the demoralization of the Jewish people. Through his leadership, the walls are rebuilt, symbolizing the restoration of the community's safety and spirit.

UPRIGHT KEYWORDS:	REVERSED KEYWORDS:
Leadership	Suppressed Feelings
Balance	Control
Wisdom	Instability
Stability	Neglect
Vision	Resistance

Upright: This card represents emotional mastery, leadership, and compassion. Like Nehemiah rebuilding Jerusalem, it reflects the ability to lead with wisdom, balancing strength and empathy. Use your emotional intelligence to inspire and guide others through challenges.

- **Leadership** – Guide others with emotional intelligence and integrity.
- **Balance** – Harmonize strength and compassion to inspire trust.
- **Wisdom** – Make decisions rooted in empathy and understanding.
- **Stability** – Create a foundation of emotional and spiritual security.
- **Vision** – Inspire others with a clear purpose and faith-driven action.

Reversed: Unresolved emotions or misuse of authority may create instability. Suppressed feelings or overcontrol hinder progress. This card encourages you to confront your emotional blocks and lead with authenticity and balance.

- **Suppressed Feelings** – Repressed emotions hinder personal and relational growth.
- **Control** – Overly rigid leadership stifles connection and trust.
- **Instability** – Emotional imbalance disrupts your ability to lead effectively.
- **Neglect** – Ignoring personal needs weakens your foundation.
- **Resistance** – Avoiding vulnerability blocks authentic connections.

Ace of Feathers

SAUL'S CONVERSION

He fell to the ground and heard a voice say to him,
"Saul, Saul, why do you persecute Me?"
Acts 9:4 BSB

ACE of FEATHERS
SAUL'S CONVERSION (ACTS 9)

Saul, known for persecuting early Christians, experiences a divine intervention while on his way to Damascus to arrest more followers of Jesus. A blinding light from heaven strikes him down, and he hears the voice of Jesus asking, "Saul, Saul, why do you persecute me?" Temporarily blinded, Saul is led into Damascus, where Ananias, a disciple, is instructed by God to heal him. Saul's sight is restored, he is baptized, and filled with the Holy Spirit. He begins to preach that Jesus is the Son of God, marking a complete transformation from persecutor to apostle, and becomes known as Paul.

UPRIGHT KEYWORDS:	REVERSED KEYWORDS:
Awakening	Confusion
Truth	Resistance
Transformation	Denial
Insight	Miscommunication
Determination	Stagnation

Upright: This card symbolizes a powerful awakening and transformation. Like Saul's conversion on the road to Damascus, it represents clarity, insight, and a new perspective that reshapes your beliefs. It calls for honesty, intellectual breakthroughs, and the courage to embrace profound change in your life.

- **Awakening** – A moment of clarity that reshapes your beliefs.
- **Truth** – Confronting inner realities to align with your higher purpose.
- **Transformation** – A profound shift opens the path for spiritual growth.
- **Insight** – New perspectives illuminate solutions to challenges.
- **Determination** – Taking decisive action toward personal growth.

Reversed: Resistance to change clouds your vision, leaving you stuck in outdated beliefs or confusion. Fear of confronting hard truths blocks clarity and growth. This card warns against avoiding transformative insights and urges you to open yourself to the potential of a new mindset.

- **Confusion** – Struggling to see the truth or gain clarity.
- **Resistance** – Avoiding necessary changes or new perspectives.
- **Denial** – Refusing to acknowledge deeper truths.
- **Miscommunication** – Failing to articulate or understand inner needs.
- **Stagnation** – Fear of change prevents progress.

Two of Feathers

GOD TESTS ABRAHAM'S FAITH

"Take your son," God said, "your only son Isaac, whom you love, and go to the land of Moriah. Offer him there as a burnt offering on one of the mountains, which I will show you."
Genesis 22:2 BSB

TWO *of* FEATHERS
GOD TESTS ABRAHAM'S FAITH (GENESIS 22)

God tests Abraham's faith by asking him to sacrifice his son Isaac as a burnt offering. Despite the unimaginable emotional turmoil this request causes, Abraham prepares to obey God's command. However, as Abraham raises his knife, an angel of the Lord intervenes, stopping him and providing a ram as an alternative sacrifice. This test demonstrates Abraham's unwavering faith and obedience to God, and it reinforces the covenant between God and Abraham's descendants.

UPRIGHT KEYWORDS:	REVERSED KEYWORDS:
Decision	Indecision
Balance	Conflict
Trust	Avoidance
Clarity	Doubt
Resolve	Imbalance

Upright: This card reflects a difficult decision requiring trust in divine guidance. Like Abraham's test of faith, it calls for balance, introspection, and moral clarity. It represents the challenge of weighing conflicting choices while remaining aligned with your higher purpose.

- **Decision** – A pivotal choice tests your faith and courage.
- **Balance** – Weighing options to find alignment with your values.
- **Trust** – Leaning on divine wisdom during moments of doubt.
- **Clarity** – Discerning the right path amid uncertainty.
- **Resolve** – Facing difficult choices with conviction.

Reversed: Indecision and self-doubt paralyze your ability to move forward. Fear of making the wrong choice leads to avoidance and inner conflict. This card urges you to confront the uncertainty and trust in divine wisdom to guide you through challenging decisions.

- **Indecision** – Paralysis from fear of making the wrong choice.
- **Conflict** – Inner turmoil disrupts emotional and mental clarity.
- **Avoidance** – Evading responsibility leads to stagnation.
- **Doubt** – A lack of trust in your intuition or divine guidance.
- **Imbalance** – Struggling to reconcile conflicting priorities.

Three of Feathers

BETRAYAL OF A SON: ABSALOM'S REVOLT

The king was shaken and went up to the chamber over the gate and wept. And as he walked, he cried out, "O my son Absalom! My son, my son Absalom! If only I had died instead of you, O Absalom, my son, my son!"
2 Samuel 18:33 BSB

THREE *of* FEATHERS
BETRAYAL OF A SON: ABSALOM'S REVOLT (2 SAMUEL 18:33)

Absalom, King David's son, rebels against his father in an attempt to usurp the throne, leading to civil war in Israel. Despite the betrayal and conflict, David orders his generals to deal gently with Absalom. However, in the heat of battle, Absalom is killed. When David hears of his son's death, he is overwhelmed with grief, mourning deeply for Absalom and wishing he had died in his son's place. This moment underscores the profound pain of personal loss and the heartache stemming from family conflict and betrayal.

UPRIGHT KEYWORDS:	REVERSED KEYWORDS:
Heartbreak	Suppression
Betrayal	Bitterness
Sorrow	Isolation
Reflection	Denial
Reconciliation	Stagnation

Upright: This card signifies heartbreak, betrayal, and the pain of conflict. Like the rebellion against David, it reflects emotional wounds caused by division and loss. It encourages you to confront this pain, allowing space for healing and eventual reconciliation.

- **Heartbreak** – Painful experiences open the door for healing.
- **Betrayal** – Facing the impact of broken trust.
- **Sorrow** – Acknowledging emotional wounds for growth.
- **Reflection** – Gaining wisdom from difficult experiences.
- **Reconciliation** – Opportunities for healing and forgiveness.

Reversed: Suppressed grief or unresolved betrayal deepens inner turmoil. Avoidance of emotional pain prolongs suffering and prevents closure. This card warns against ignoring wounds and encourages you to address them to begin the process of healing.

- **Suppression** – Avoiding emotional pain prolongs suffering.
- **Bitterness** – Holding onto past wounds hinders progress.
- **Isolation** – Allowing heartbreak to disconnect you from others.
- **Denial** – Refusing to face the root causes of grief.
- **Stagnation** – Unresolved emotions block healing.

Four of Feathers

ELIJAH'S RETREAT INTO SILENCE

After the earthquake there was a fire, but the LORD was not in the fire. And after the fire came a still, small voice.
1 Kings 19:12 BSB

FOUR *of* FEATHERS
ELIJAH'S RETREAT INTO SILENCE (1 KINGS 19:9-18)

After a significant victory at Mount Carmel, where Elijah demonstrates God's power over the prophets of Baal, Jezebel threatens Elijah's life, causing him to flee into the wilderness. Feeling defeated and isolated, Elijah seeks refuge in a cave on Mount Horeb. There God speaks to Elijah in a "gentle whisper," providing him with guidance, comfort, and the strength to continue his prophetic mission. This moment of quiet reflection and divine encounter highlights the importance of solitude and rest for spiritual clarity and renewal.

UPRIGHT KEYWORDS:	REVERSED KEYWORDS:
Rest	Exhaustion
Rejuvenation	Avoidance
Solitude	Overwhelm
Clarity	Disconnection
Renewal	Procrastination

Upright: This card represents rest, introspection, and spiritual renewal. Like Elijah retreating in silence, it invites you to step back from conflict and seek inner peace. It signifies a time for recovery and reflection to prepare for what lies ahead

- **Rest** – A period of recovery and self-reflection.
- **Rejuvenation** – Restoring energy to prepare for future challenges.
- **Solitude** – Seeking peace through quiet introspection.
- **Clarity** – Finding answers in stillness and silence.
- **Renewal** – Gaining strength through spiritual retreat.

Reversed: Avoiding the need for rest leads to burnout and stagnation. Overwhelm from constant mental or emotional strain prevents healing. This card urges you to prioritize self-care and take the necessary time for quiet reflection and rejuvenation.

- **Exhaustion** – Ignoring the need for rest leads to burnout.
- **Avoidance** – Using withdrawal to escape responsibilities.
- **Overwhelm** – Feeling unable to find peace amid chaos.
- **Disconnection** – Struggling to reconnect with your inner self.
- **Procrastination** – Delaying action due to fear of engagement.

Five of Feathers

KING SAUL'S TRAGIC DOWNFALL

*The LORD has torn the kingdom out of your hand
and given it to your neighbor David.*
1 Samuel 28:17 BSB

King Saul, the first king of Israel, initially chosen by God to lead, faces a tragic downfall due to a series of disobediences and moral failures. One pivotal moment comes when God commands Saul through Samuel to destroy the Amalekites completely as divine retribution for their opposition to Israel. Saul, however, spares the king of the Amalekites, and the best of their livestock. Samuel confronts Saul and announces God's rejection of Saul as king. This event marks the beginning of Saul's decline, highlighting the dangers of disobedience, pride, and the prioritization of personal desires over divine commands.

FIVE *of* FEATHERS
KING SAUL'S TRAGIC DOWNFALL (1 SAMUEL 15)

UPRIGHT KEYWORDS:	REVERSED KEYWORDS:
Conflict	Regret
Pride	Stubbornness
Loss	Isolation
Humility	Self-Sabotage
Introspection	Forgiveness

Upright: This card reflects conflict, loss, and the consequences of pride. Like Saul's downfall, it warns against selfishness or destructive behavior that leads to isolation. It calls for humility and introspection to find lessons within defeat and rebuild with wisdom.

- **Conflict** – Navigating challenges in relationships or goals.
- **Pride** – Recognizing the cost of arrogance or self-interest.
- **Loss** – Accepting the lessons of defeat.
- **Humility** – Learning to grow from setbacks.
- **Introspection** – Reflecting on the causes of failure to rebuild stronger.

Reversed: Lingering regret or unresolved guilt creates a cycle of negativity. Refusal to take accountability deepens inner conflict. This card encourages you to face your mistakes, release past failures, and seek forgiveness to move forward.

- **Regret** – Lingering guilt prevents moving forward.
- **Stubbornness** – Refusal to learn from mistakes perpetuates conflict.
- **Isolation** – Pushing others away through defensiveness or blame.
- **Self-Sabotage** – Allowing pride to block progress.
- **Forgiveness** – Struggling to release resentment or blame.

Six of Feathers

RUTH THE MOABITE

*"Do not urge me to leave you or to turn from following you.
For wherever you go, I will go, and wherever you live, I will live;
your people will be my people, and your God will be my God.*
Ruth 1:16 BSB

SIX of FEATHERS
RUTH THE MOABITE (RUTH 1:6-22)

Following the deaths of her sons, Naomi decides to leave Moab and return to Bethlehem. She urges her daughters-in-law, Orpah and Ruth, to remain in Moab and remarry. Orpah eventually stays, but Ruth clings to Naomi, famously declaring, "Where you go I will go, and where you stay I will stay. Your people will be my people and your God my God." Ruth's loyalty leads her to a new land and eventually to marriage with Boaz, a relative of Naomi's husband. Through her faithfulness and resilience, Ruth becomes the great-grandmother of King David, integrating into the lineage of Jesus.

UPRIGHT KEYWORDS:	REVERSED KEYWORDS:
Transition	Resistance
Hope	Stagnation
Support	Doubt
Healing	Disconnection
Determination	Regret

Upright: This card signifies a journey toward healing and renewal. Like Ruth's faithful transition, it represents hope, support, and the promise of a brighter future. It encourages leaving behind difficult circumstances to embrace new opportunities with trust and determination.

- **Transition** – Moving toward a new chapter in life.
- **Hope** – Trusting in the promise of brighter days.
- **Support** – Finding strength through companionship and faith.
- **Healing** – Leaving pain behind to embrace renewal.
- **Determination** – Walking forward with courage and perseverance.

Reversed: Fear of change or clinging to the past creates stagnation. Struggles with letting go hinder progress and healing. This card urges you to trust the process of moving forward, even if the path ahead feels uncertain.

- **Resistance** – Fear of change delays progress.
- **Stagnation** – Clinging to the past prevents healing.
- **Doubt** – Uncertainty clouds the way forward.
- **Disconnection** – Struggling to find emotional or spiritual support.
- **Regret** – Holding onto old wounds blocks transformation.

Seven of Feathers

JACOB THE DECEIVER

*Jacob said to his father, "I am Esau, your firstborn.
I have done as you told me. Please sit up and eat some of my game,
so that you may bless me."*
Genesis 27:19 BSB

SEVEN *of* FEATHERS
JACOB THE DECEIVER (GENESIS 27)

Isaac, who is old and blind, intends to bless his eldest son Esau, a tradition granting rights and inheritance. Rebekah, overhearing this and favoring Jacob, orchestrates a deceit: Jacob, disguised as Esau, receives Isaac's blessing by pretending to be his brother. When Esau learns of the betrayal, he is devastated, and Jacob must flee to avoid his brother's wrath. This pivotal act of deception shapes much of Jacob's future, teaching profound lessons about truth, consequence, and the complexity of familial bonds.

UPRIGHT KEYWORDS:	REVERSED KEYWORDS:
Strategy	Dishonesty
Cunning	Deception
Discernment	Paranoia
Awareness	Lack of Trust
Adaptability	Self-Sabotage

Chapter 26

Upright: This card reflects cunning, strategy, and the need for discernment. Like Jacob's deception, it warns against dishonesty while encouraging you to navigate challenges with wisdom and care. It highlights the importance of authenticity and awareness in your actions.

- *Strategy – Planning carefully to overcome challenges.*
- *Cunning – Using intellect and resourcefulness wisely.*
- *Discernment – Evaluating motives—yours and others'.*
- *Awareness – Recognizing deception or hidden truths.*
- *Adaptability – Navigating obstacles with creative solutions.*

Reversed: Deception or manipulation backfires, creating chaos and mistrust. Denying your true self or ignoring ethical concerns leads to inner conflict. This card urges you to confront dishonest behaviors and align your actions with integrity.

- **Dishonesty** – Failing to act with integrity undermines growth.
- **Deception** – Falling prey to manipulation or self-delusion.
- **Paranoia** – Allowing fear to distort perceptions.
- **Lack of Trust** – Struggling to believe in yourself or others.
- **Self-Sabotage** – Acting against your best interests creates setbacks.

Eight of Feathers

JONAH TRAPPED INSIDE THE FISH

"In my distress I called to the LORD, and He answered me. From the belly of Sheol I called for help, and You heard my voice.
Jonah 2:2 BSB

EIGHT *of* **FEATHERS**
JONAH TRAPPED INSIDE THE FISH (JONAH 2)

God commands Jonah to go to Nineveh and preach against its wickedness. Jonah, however, flees in the opposite direction, boarding a ship to Tarshish. A great storm endangers the ship, and Jonah, realizing he is the cause for the storm, asks to be thrown overboard, leading to him being swallowed by a great fish. Inside the fish for three days and nights, Jonah prays to God, repenting for his disobedience. God commands the fish to spit Jonah onto dry land, giving him a second chance to fulfill his mission. This experience transforms Jonah, teaching him about obedience, repentance, and God's mercy.

UPRIGHT KEYWORDS:	REVERSED KEYWORDS:
Restriction	Avoidance
Reflection	Fear
Surrender	Denial
Patience	Victimhood
Breakthrough	Stagnation

Upright: This card symbolizes feeling trapped or restricted by circumstances. Like Jonah in the belly of the fish, it reflects the need for surrender and reflection to find release. It encourages faith and patience as you navigate challenges and seek clarity.

- **Restriction** – Feeling confined by circumstances or inner struggles.
- **Reflection** – A time of introspection to uncover hidden truths.
- **Surrender** – Releasing resistance to allow growth.
- **Patience** – Trusting that change will come in divine timing.
- **Breakthrough** – Gaining clarity through temporary stillness.

Reversed: Resistance to change intensifies feelings of confinement. Refusal to confront the cause of your struggles prolongs stagnation. This card urges you to face what binds you and embrace the path to freedom and renewal.

- **Avoidance** – Refusing to confront what is holding you back.
- **Fear** – Allowing anxiety to amplify feelings of confinement.
- **Denial** – Resisting lessons hidden within current struggles.
- **Victimhood** – Feeling powerless instead of reclaiming agency.
- **Stagnation** – Remaining stuck by clinging to limiting beliefs.

Nine of Feathers

PETER DENIES JESUS

Then Peter remembered the word that Jesus had spoken:
"Before the rooster crows, you will deny Me three times."
And he went outside and wept bitterly.
Matthew 26:75 BSB

NINE of FEATHERS
PETER DENIES JESUS (MATTHEW 26:69-75)

Before Jesus' crucifixion, He predicts that Peter will deny Him three times before the rooster crows. Despite Peter's initial protestations of loyalty, when confronted by others, Peter denies knowing Jesus to protect himself. After the third denial, the rooster crows, and Peter remembers Jesus' words. Overwhelmed by guilt and shame, Peter weeps bitterly. This event marks a profound moment of personal failure and anguish for Peter, yet it also sets the stage for his later redemption and leadership in the early Christian community.

UPRIGHT KEYWORDS:	REVERSED KEYWORDS:
Guilt	Shame
Fear	Avoidance
Reflection	Isolation
Compassion	Hopelessness
Redemption	Denial

Upright: This card reflects guilt, fear, and inner conflict. Like Peter's denial, it highlights the weight of personal regret and the need for forgiveness. It encourages self-compassion and a willingness to confront mistakes as part of the healing process.

- **Guilt** – Acknowledging past mistakes and seeking forgiveness.
- **Fear** – Recognizing the influence of anxiety on your decisions.
- **Reflection** – Understanding the deeper roots of regret.
- **Compassion** – Learning to forgive yourself and others.
- **Redemption** – Finding healing through honest self-awareness.

Reversed: Unresolved guilt or fear overwhelms your ability to move forward. Avoidance of responsibility deepens inner turmoil. This card calls you to face your shadows, forgive yourself, and embrace the possibility of redemption.

- **Shame** – Suppressing guilt leads to deeper emotional distress.
- **Avoidance** – Refusing to confront the consequences of your actions.
- **Isolation** – Pulling away from others out of fear of judgment.
- **Hopelessness** – Believing mistakes define your worth.
- **Denial** – Blocking opportunities for healing and forgiveness.

Ten of Feathers

SAMSON LOSES HIS STRENGTH

And having lulled him to sleep on her lap,
she called a man to shave off the seven braids of his head.
In this way she began to subdue him, and his strength left him.
Judges 16:19 BSB

Samson, granted extraordinary strength by God, becomes vulnerable through his love for Delilah. The Philistine rulers bribe Delilah to discover the source of Samson's strength. After three failed attempts, she finally coaxes the secret from him: his uncut hair, a symbol of his vow to God. While he sleeps, Delilah has his hair cut, and Samson's strength leaves him. The Philistines capture, blind, and imprison him. However, in his final act, Samson calls upon God, and his strength is temporarily restored, allowing him to bring down the temple of Dagon, dying, but achieving a posthumous victory.

UPRIGHT KEYWORDS:	REVERSED KEYWORDS:
Endings	Resistance
Surrender	Despair
Transformation	Victimhood
Release	Stagnation
Resilience	Self-Sabotage

Upright: This card represents the end of a cycle and the pain of loss. Like Samson's fall, it signifies the consequences of overconfidence or betrayal. It encourages acceptance of endings as a prelude to renewal and transformation.

- **Endings** – The closure of a difficult chapter allows for renewal.
- **Surrender** – Accepting the loss of old patterns to rebuild anew.
- **Transformation** – Painful experiences pave the way for growth.
- **Release** – Letting go of what no longer serves you.
- **Resilience** – Finding strength in recovery and renewal.

Reversed: Resistance to endings prolongs suffering and delays growth. Fear of change or refusal to accept reality creates stagnation. This card urges you to release what no longer serves you and trust in the opportunity for rebirth.

- **Resistance** – Refusing to accept necessary endings delays healing.
- **Despair** – Feeling overwhelmed by loss or betrayal.
- **Victimhood** – Focusing on defeat rather than opportunities to rebuild.
- **Stagnation** – Fear of starting over keeps you stuck.
- **Self-Sabotage** – Clinging to old ways despite their destructive impact.

Page of Feathers

ESTHER SAVES THE JEWS

*Queen Esther replied, "If I have found favor in your sight, O king,
and if it pleases the king, grant me my life as my petition,
and the lives of my people as my request.*
Esther 7:3 BSB

PAGE of FEATHERS
ESTHER SAVES THE JEWS (ESTHER 8)

Esther, a Jewish woman who becomes queen of Persia without revealing her ethnicity, discovers a plot by Haman, the king's advisor, to exterminate the Jewish people. Esther courageously plans a banquet for King Ahasuerus and Haman, where she reveals her Jewish identity and exposes Haman's plot. Moved by Esther's plea, the king orders Haman's execution. Esther's wise and brave actions lead to the issuing of a new decree that allows the Jews to defend themselves, saving them from annihilation.

UPRIGHT KEYWORDS:	REVERSED KEYWORDS:
Courage	Hesitation
Intelligence	Insecurity
Voice	Impulsiveness
Initiative	Missed Opportunities
Empowerment	Silence

Upright: This card symbolizes courage, initiative, and the power of communication. Like Esther's bold actions, it reflects the ability to stand up for truth and justice. It encourages you to take decisive steps toward creating positive change.

- **Courage** – Acting boldly to create positive change.
- **Intelligence** – Using insight and strategy to overcome challenges.
- **Voice** – Speaking your truth with clarity and confidence.
- **Initiative** – Taking the first steps toward transformation.
- **Empowerment** – Recognizing your ability to influence outcomes.

Reversed: Fear of speaking out or acting on your convictions leads to missed opportunities. Doubt in your abilities hinders progress. This card urges you to overcome fear and step into your role as a voice for change.

- **Hesitation** – Fear of speaking out or taking action creates stagnation.
- **Insecurity** – Doubts about your abilities undermine confidence.
- **Impulsiveness** – Acting without reflection leads to instability.
- **Missed Opportunities** – Avoiding responsibility blocks growth.
- **Silence** – Suppressing your voice hinders personal and collective change.

Knight of Feathers

PAUL THE APOSTLE

Saul promptly began to proclaim Jesus in the synagogues, declaring, "He is the Son of God."
Acts 9:20 BSB

KNIGHT of FEATHERS
PAUL THE APOSTLE (ACTS 28:31)

Paul, originally named Saul, begins as a persecutor of Christians, zealous in his efforts to uphold Jewish law. On the road to Damascus, intending to arrest more Christians, he is struck by a blinding light and hears the voice of Jesus. This encounter leads to Paul's conversion, after which he becomes one of Christianity's most influential apostles. He undertakes several missionary journeys, faces persecution, and writes many letters that form a significant part of the New Testament, spreading the Christian message with unparalleled zeal and intellectual argumentation.

UPRIGHT KEYWORDS:	REVERSED KEYWORDS:
Focus	Impulsiveness
Courage	Rigidity
Conviction	Conflict
Action	Doubt
Integrity	Misalignment

Upright: This card represents bold action and unwavering focus. Like Paul's determination, it reflects the courage to pursue your mission with clarity and conviction. It calls for decisive action and the pursuit of truth with determination.

- **Focus** – Pursuing goals with determination and clarity.
- **Courage** – Acting boldly in alignment with your values.
- **Conviction** – Staying true to your purpose despite opposition.
- **Action** – Moving forward with decisive energy.
- **Integrity** – Leading with honesty and unwavering principles.

Reversed: Impulsiveness or recklessness disrupts your progress. Acting without reflection creates instability and conflict. This card urges you to temper your drive with wisdom and ensure your actions align with your higher purpose.

- **Impulsiveness** – Acting without careful thought leads to setbacks.
- **Rigidity** – Holding onto ideas too tightly blocks progress.
- **Conflict** – Aggression or rash behavior creates discord.
- **Doubt** – Questioning your path undermines your momentum.
- **Misalignment** – Pursuing goals without integrity weakens your foundation.

Queen of Feathers

ABIGAIL THE PEACEMAKER

Blessed is your discernment, and blessed are you,
because today you kept me from bloodshed
and from avenging myself by my own hand.
1 Samuel 25:33 BSB

QUEEN of FEATHERS
ABIGAIL THE PEACEMAKER (1 SAMUEL 25)

Abigail, the wife of Nabal, a wealthy but harsh man, intervenes to prevent bloodshed between her husband and David. After Nabal insultingly refuses to provide food to David and his men, despite their protection of his flock, David vows revenge. Abigail, learning of the impending danger, quickly gathers provisions and sets off to meet David. She offers the supplies and pleads for peace, appealing to David's better nature and his future as king of Israel. Her wisdom and eloquence persuade David to abandon his vengeful plan. Abigail's actions demonstrate remarkable diplomatic acumen and moral integrity.

UPRIGHT KEYWORDS:	REVERSED KEYWORDS:
Diplomacy	Overextension
Compassion	Avoidance
Strength	Resentment
Clarity	Instability
Balance	Isolation

Upright: This card embodies wisdom, diplomacy, and the ability to bring harmony to conflict. Like Abigail, it reflects the power of gentle yet firm communication to resolve tensions. It encourages leading with compassion and emotional intelligence.

- **Diplomacy** – Resolving conflict with wisdom and grace.
- **Compassion** – Understanding others' perspectives fosters harmony.
- **Strength** – Leading with calm confidence during challenges.
- **Clarity** – Bringing reason and insight to emotional situations.
- **Balance** – Maintaining peace while honoring your own boundaries.

Reversed: Avoidance of conflict or overextension in maintaining peace leads to imbalance. Suppressing your needs to appease others creates resentment. This card calls for setting boundaries and addressing tensions with honesty and care.

- **Overextension** – Taking on too much to maintain peace leads to burnout.
- **Avoidance** – Suppressing your needs to avoid conflict causes imbalance.
- **Resentment** – Neglecting self-care creates frustration and strain.
- **Instability** – Struggling to mediate or resolve tensions effectively.
- **Isolation** – Withdrawing from challenges rather than addressing them.

King of Feathers

THE JUDGMENT OF SOLOMON

Then the king gave his ruling:
"Give the living baby to the first woman.
By no means should you kill him; she is his mother."
1 Kings 3:27 BSB

KING *of* FEATHERS
THE JUDGEMENT OF SOLOMON (1 KINGS 3:16-28)

Two women come before King Solomon, each claiming to be the mother of a baby. Solomon suggests cutting the baby in half, each woman to receive half. One woman agrees to the division, but the other, the true mother, pleads for the baby's life, offering to relinquish her claim so that her child may live. Solomon, discerning the true mother's compassion, awards her the baby, demonstrating unparalleled wisdom and understanding of human nature. This story highlights Solomon's ability to govern with insight and justice, earning him a reputation for wisdom.

UPRIGHT KEYWORDS:	REVERSED KEYWORDS:
Wisdom	Bias
Leadership	Abuse of Power
Justice	Instability
Authority	Neglect
Insight	Disconnection

Upright: This card symbolizes wisdom, fairness, and discernment in leadership. Like Solomon's judgment, it reflects the ability to make balanced decisions that align with truth and justice. It encourages you to guide others with integrity and clarity.

- **Wisdom** – Making balanced decisions rooted in integrity and fairness.
- **Leadership** – Guiding others with clarity and empathy.
- **Justice** – Acting as a moral compass in challenging situations.
- **Authority** – Using power responsibly to foster trust.
- **Insight** – Seeing beyond appearances to discern deeper truths.

Reversed: Misuse of power or biased decision-making creates discord. Ignoring ethical responsibilities leads to instability and mistrust. This card urges you to align your choices with honesty and fairness to restore harmony.

- **Bias** – Allowing personal interests to cloud judgment.
- **Abuse of Power** – Misusing authority erodes trust and stability.
- **Instability** – Difficulty making balanced or ethical decisions.
- **Neglect** – Failing to fulfill responsibilities with fairness and care.
- **Disconnection** – Ignoring the emotional or moral impact of your actions.

Ace of Grains

ENTERING THE PROMISED LAND

*I have given you every place where the sole of your foot will tread,
just as I promised to Moses.*
Joshua 1:3 BSB

ACE *of* GRAINS
ENTERING THE PROMISED LAND (JOSHUA 1:1-9)

After the death of Moses, Joshua is appointed by God to lead the Israelites into the Promised Land. God commands Joshua to be strong and courageous, promising to be with him as he was with Moses. Joshua is to lead the people across the Jordan River into the land God has promised to their ancestors. This marks a new beginning for the Israelites, a fulfillment of God's promise of a land flowing with milk and honey. It signifies not just a physical relocation but a spiritual inheritance, a foundation upon which the future of the Israelite nation is to be built.

UPRIGHT KEYWORDS:	REVERSED KEYWORDS:
Abundance	Missed Opportunities
Potential	Lack
Blessings	Stagnation
Beginnings	Resistance
Foundation	Imbalance

Upright: This card represents new beginnings, prosperity, and divine blessings. Like entering the Promised Land, it signifies a time of abundance and the fulfillment of God's promises. Embrace opportunities for material and spiritual growth with gratitude and faith in the divine plan.

- **Abundance** – A new phase of material and spiritual prosperity begins.
- **Potential** – Seeds of opportunity promise growth and fulfillment.
- **Blessings** – Divine gifts invite gratitude and trust in the future.
- **Beginnings** – A fresh start grounded in faith and purpose.
- **Foundation** – Building a secure base for long-term success.

Reversed: Missed opportunities or reluctance to embrace blessings create stagnation. Fear of change or self-doubt may block prosperity and growth. This card urges you to trust in divine provision and overcome resistance to entering a new chapter of abundance.

- **Missed Opportunities** – Fear of change prevents progress.
- **Lack** – Neglecting blessings creates feelings of scarcity.
- **Stagnation** – Failure to act on opportunities halts growth.
- **Resistance** – Reluctance to embrace new beginnings delays transformation.
- **Imbalance** – Overemphasis on material pursuits disconnects you from your spiritual path.

Two of Grains

LYDIA - FAITHFUL BUSINESSWOMAN

Among those listening was a woman named Lydia, a dealer in purple cloth from the city of Thyatira, who was a worshiper of God. The Lord opened her heart to respond to Paul's message.
Acts 16:14 BSB

TWO *of* GRAINS
LYDIA - FAITHFUL BUSINESSWOMAN (ACTS 16:14-16)

Lydia, a seller of purple cloth in Philippi, meets Paul and his companions during their missionary travels. She is described as a worshiper of God, and upon hearing Paul's message, she and her household are baptized, embracing Christianity. Demonstrating hospitality and support for Paul's mission, Lydia invites them into her home, providing a base for their work in the city. Her story illustrates the successful integration of professional success and personal faith, showing how her resources and influence support the early Christian community.

UPRIGHT KEYWORDS:	REVERSED KEYWORDS:
Balance	Overwhelm
Adaptability	Disconnection
Faith	Procrastination
Partnership	Stress
Flow	Scattered Focus

Upright: This card reflects balance and adaptability in managing life's responsibilities. Like Lydia, it encourages you to align your work with faith, maintaining harmony between material success and spiritual values. Stay flexible and trust your ability to manage competing priorities.

- **Balance** – Managing responsibilities with grace and focus.
- **Adaptability** – Staying flexible in the face of shifting priorities.
- **Faith** – Aligning material pursuits with spiritual values.
- **Partnership** – Harmonizing relationships and teamwork in your endeavors.
- **Flow** – Skillfully juggling competing demands with trust and confidence.

Reversed: Imbalance or neglect of spiritual values may disrupt harmony in your life. Struggling to juggle responsibilities creates stress and disconnection. This card urges you to reassess priorities and find equilibrium between work and faith.

- **Overwhelm** – Struggling to manage responsibilities leads to chaos.
- **Disconnection** – Imbalance disrupts harmony between work and spiritual life.
- **Procrastination** – Avoiding decisions prevents forward movement.
- **Stress** – Overcommitting creates strain and exhaustion.
- **Scattered Focus** – Difficulty prioritizing hinders success and clarity.

Three of Grains

BUILDING SOLOMON'S TEMPLE

"As for this temple you are building, if you walk in My statutes, carry out My ordinances, and keep all My commandments by walking in them, I will fulfill through you the promise I made to your father David.
1 Kings 6:12 BSB

THREE of GRAINS
BUILDING SOLOMON'S TEMPLE (1 KINGS 6)

Solomon embarks on the ambitious project of building the temple to house the Ark of the Covenant, fulfilling a divine mandate and his father David's dream. The construction involves skilled artisans, vast resources, and detailed planning, reflecting Solomon's commitment to creating a magnificent space for worship. It symbolizes not only religious devotion but also the power of collective endeavor and expert craftsmanship. The temple's completion after seven years stands as a testament to Solomon's wisdom, the workers' skill, and the nation's collective effort.

UPRIGHT KEYWORDS:	REVERSED KEYWORDS:
Collaboration	Disconnection
Craftsmanship	Neglect
Dedication	Frustration
Purpose	Conflict
Progress	Stagnation

Upright: This card signifies collaboration, craftsmanship, and pur-poseful work. Like building Solomon's Temple, it represents the value of teamwork and dedication to achieving great goals. Align your efforts with divine purpose to create something enduring and meaningful.

- **Collaboration** – Working together toward a shared vision brings success.
- **Craftsmanship** – Honing your skills with purpose and care.
- **Dedication** – Commitment to meaningful work fosters spiritual and material growth.
- **Purpose** – Aligning efforts with divine intent creates lasting impact.
- **Progress** – Steady advancement in building something significant.

Reversed: Disconnection or lack of coordination in teamwork hinders progress. Neglecting to align your efforts with higher purpose creates frustration. This card encourages you to rebuild collaboration and refocus on your spiritual and material goals.

- **Disconnection** – Lack of teamwork or misaligned goals hinders progress.
- **Neglect** – Failure to nurture your talents stalls growth.
- **Frustration** – Feeling stuck in your work diminishes motivation.
- **Conflict** – Miscommunication disrupts harmony in collaboration.
- **Stagnation** – Avoiding responsibility blocks meaningful progress.

Four of Grains

PARABLE OF THE RICH FOOL

And He said to them,
"Watch out! Guard yourselves against every form of greed, for
one's life does not consist in the abundance of his possessions."
Luke 12:15 BSB

FOUR *of* GRAINS
PARABLE OF THE RICH FOOL (LUKE 12:13-21)

Jesus tells the parable of a rich man who, after a bountiful harvest, decides to tear down his barns to build larger ones to store all his grain and goods. He believes this will secure his future, allowing him to relax, eat, drink, and be merry. However, God calls him a fool because his life is demanded of him that very night, and he cannot take his wealth with him after death. The parable concludes with the lesson that this is how it will be for anyone who stores up treasures for themselves but is not rich toward God.

UPRIGHT KEYWORDS:	REVERSED KEYWORDS:
Security	Greed
Gratitude	Insecurity
Stewardship	Isolation
Boundaries	Stagnation
Reflection	Hoarding

Upright: This card reflects security and the need for wise stewardship. Like the rich fool, it reminds you to guard against hoarding wealth without purpose. Embrace gratitude and generosity to balance material stability with spiritual fulfillment.

- **Security** – Finding stability through careful management of resources.
- **Gratitude** – Appreciating blessings without attachment.
- **Stewardship** – Responsibly managing material and spiritual wealth.
- **Boundaries** – Protecting what matters most with wisdom and care.
- **Reflection** – Balancing material desires with deeper values.

Reversed: Greed or fear of loss may create emotional or material stagnation. Overattachment to possessions leads to emptiness. This card warns against prioritizing wealth over relationships and spiritual values, encouraging generosity and trust in divine provision.

- **Greed** – Overattachment to possessions disrupts emotional and spiritual growth.
- **Insecurity** – Fear of loss prevents joy and generosity.
- **Isolation** – Holding on too tightly creates disconnection from others.
- **Stagnation** – Refusal to share or invest leads to unfulfilled potential.
- **Hoarding** – Accumulating without purpose erodes inner fulfillment.

Five of Grains

THE BLEEDING WOMAN

She said to herself,
"If only I touch His cloak, I will be healed."
Matthew 9:21 BSB

FIVE of GRAINS
THE BLEEDING WOMAN (MATTHEW 9:20-22)

The story tells of a woman who had been bleeding for twelve years, a condition that made her ritually unclean and isolated her from society. Despite spending all she had on treatments without improvement, her situation only worsened. Hearing about Jesus, she approaches Him in a crowd, believing that touching His cloak would heal her. Her faith is rewarded; she touches His garment and is instantly healed. Jesus turns to her and acknowledges her faith, saying, "Daughter, your faith has healed you. Go in peace and be freed from your suffering."

UPRIGHT KEYWORDS:	REVERSED KEYWORDS:
Struggle	Despair
Vulnerability	Avoidance
Support	Fear
Faith	Dependency
Resilience	Resistance

Upright: This card represents hardship, vulnerability, and the path to healing. Like the bleeding woman who touched Jesus' cloak, it reminds you that faith and courage can lead to restoration. Seek support and remain hopeful as you navigate difficulties.

- **Struggle** – Acknowledging challenges as part of the healing process.
- **Vulnerability** – Finding strength through faith during hardships.
- **Support** – Seeking and accepting help to overcome obstacles.
- **Faith** – Trusting in divine guidance for renewal and growth.
- **Resilience** – Perseverance leads to eventual healing and transformation.

Reversed: Isolation and despair deepen feelings of lack or struggle. Refusing to seek help or confront pain prolongs suffering. This card urges you to have faith in the healing process and reach out for the support you need.

- **Despair** – Focusing on lack deepens feelings of isolation.
- **Avoidance** – Refusing to address pain delays healing.
- **Fear** – Doubting the possibility of recovery blocks progress.
- **Dependency** – Overreliance on external validation weakens self-reliance.
- **Resistance** – Refusing to let go of suffering hinders growth.

Six of Grains

WIDOW'S GENEROSITY

Jesus called His disciples to Him and said,
"Truly I tell you, this poor widow has put more
than all the others into the treasury.
Mark 12:43 BSB

SIX of GRAINS
WIDOW'S GENEROSITY (MARK 12:41-44)

Jesus observes people offering money at the temple and notices a poor widow who contributes just a couple small coins, worth very little. He tells His disciples that this widow has given more than all the others making contributions because they gave out of their wealth, but she, out of her poverty, put in everything she had, all she had to live on. This act of selfless giving demonstrates true generosity and sacrifice, contrasting with those who give only from their surplus.

UPRIGHT KEYWORDS:	REVERSED KEYWORDS:
Kindness	Scarcity
Generosity	Selfishness
Balance	Imbalance
Trust	Resentment
Harmony	Disconnection

Upright: This card reflects giving, kindness, and trust in divine provision. Like the widow's generosity, it reminds you that small acts of selflessness can have profound impact. Share your blessings with others, trusting that your needs will be met through faith.

- **Kindness** – Giving selflessly fosters emotional and spiritual abundance.
- **Generosity** – Sharing your blessings builds trust and connection.
- **Balance** – Receiving with gratitude complements acts of giving.
- **Trust** – Belief in divine provision alleviates fear of scarcity.
- **Harmony** – Aligning material actions with spiritual values creates peace.

Reversed: Fear of scarcity prevents you from sharing or receiving blessings. Selfishness or mistrust disrupts harmony and abundance. This card encourages you to release fear and embrace the flow of generosity and gratitude.

- **Scarcity** – Fear of lack prevents acts of generosity.
- **Selfishness** – Prioritizing personal gain disrupts harmony.
- **Imbalance** – Overgiving drains your emotional or material resources.
- **Resentment** – Feeling unappreciated diminishes the joy of giving.
- **Disconnection** – Avoiding vulnerability in sharing hinders meaningful relationships.

Seven of Grains

PARABLE OF THE SOWER

*Others fell on good soil
and yielded fruit: some one hundred times as much,
some sixty, and some thirty.*
Matthew 13:8 WEB

SEVEN *of* GRAINS
PARABLE OF THE SOWER (MATTHEW 13:1-23)

Jesus tells a parable about a sower who scatters seeds. Some seeds fall on the path and are eaten by birds. Some fall on rocky ground and, though they sprout quickly, they wither under the sun's heat because they have no root. Other seeds fall among thorns, which grow up and choke the plants. Finally, some seeds fall on good soil, where they produce a crop multiple times what was sown. Jesus explains that the seeds represent the word of God and the various types of ground symbolize different responses from those who hear the word.

UPRIGHT KEYWORDS:	REVERSED KEYWORDS:
Patience	Impatience
Effort	Neglect
Reflection	Misjudgment
Potential	Doubt
Faith	Waste

Upright: This card signifies patience, growth, and the fruits of hard work. Like the parable of the sower, it reminds you that careful nurturing leads to abundance. Trust in divine timing as you invest in your goals and await the harvest.

- **Patience** – Trusting the process as growth unfolds in divine timing.
- **Effort** – Diligent work is required to nurture meaningful results.
- **Reflection** – Assessing where your energy and resources are being invested.
- **Potential** – Recognizing the seeds of success within your efforts.
- **Faith** – Believing that your work will bear fruit in due time.

Reversed: Impatience or lack of effort hinders growth and success. Neglecting to nurture your goals disrupts progress. This card encourages reflection on where your energy is being invested and how to realign with purposeful effort.

- **Impatience** – Frustration at delayed outcomes blocks progress.
- **Neglect** – Failing to care for your efforts prevents growth.
- **Misjudgment** – Investing energy in unproductive paths.
- **Doubt** – Losing faith in the process creates stagnation.
- **Waste** – Squandering opportunities or resources hinders success.

Eight of Grains

THE CRAFTSMEN

*"So Bezalel, Oholiab, and every skilled person are to carry out everything
commanded by the LORD, who has given them skill and ability to know
how to perform all the work of constructing the sanctuary."*
Exodus 36:1 BSB

EIGHT *of* GRAINS
THE CRAFTSMEN (EXODUS 31)

God instructs Moses to construct a Tabernacle as a dwelling place for His presence among the Israelites during their journey through the desert. Bezalel of the tribe of Judah and Oholiab of the tribe of Dan are filled with the Spirit of God, granting them wisdom, understanding, and skill in all kinds of crafts. They, along with other skilled artisans, are tasked with building the Tabernacle and its furnishings according to precise specifications given by God. This work not only requires technical skill but also spiritual dedication, as it serves a holy purpose.

UPRIGHT KEYWORDS:	REVERSED KEYWORDS:
Dedication	Perfectionism
Skill	Distraction
Purpose	Neglect
Progress	Frustration
Discipline	Stagnation

Upright: This card represents dedication, skill, and craftsmanship. Like Bezalel and Oholiab, it reflects the value of honing your talents to create something meaningful. Focus on your work with care and intention, trusting that your efforts will bear fruit.

- **Dedication** – Mastering your craft through focused effort and intention.
- **Skill** – Developing talents to create something meaningful.
- **Purpose** – Aligning work with divine intent brings fulfillment.
- **Progress** – Tangible advancements result from consistent effort.
- **Discipline** – Commitment to excellence drives success and growth.

Reversed: Perfectionism or lack of focus disrupts your progress. Neglecting your gifts or pursuing work without purpose leads to frustration. This card urges you to reconnect with your passion and invest your energy wisely.

- **Perfectionism** – Unrealistic standards block satisfaction and completion.
- **Distraction** – Lack of focus disrupts progress and purpose.
- **Neglect** – Failing to hone your skills prevents meaningful outcomes.
- **Frustration** – Struggles with your work create emotional strain.
- **Stagnation** – Losing motivation delays personal and spiritual growth.

Nine of Grains

QUEEN OF SHEBA VISITS SOLOMON

Then she gave the king 120 talents of gold, a great quantity of spices, and precious stones. Never again were spices in such abundance brought in as those the queen of Sheba gave to King Solomon.
1 Kings 10:10 BSB

NINE *of* GRAINS
QUEEN OF SHEBA VISITS SOLOMON (1 KINGS 10)

The Queen of Sheba hears of Solomon's fame and wisdom, which she finds hard to believe, so she decides to visit Jerusalem to test him with hard questions. Solomon answers all her questions, and nothing remains hidden from him. She is overwhelmed by his wisdom, the prosperity of his kingdom, and the happiness of his subjects. Recognizing his wisdom and the blessings of his God, she gifts him gold, spices, and precious stones. Solomon, in turn, grants the queen everything she desires. The visit exemplifies mutual respect and the sharing of wealth and wisdom between two great rulers.

UPRIGHT KEYWORDS:	REVERSED KEYWORDS:
Abundance	Superficiality
Wisdom	Isolation
Independence	Greed
Fulfillment	Discontent
Appreciation	Neglect

Upright: This card reflects prosperity, wisdom, and the rewards of faith. Like the Queen of Sheba's visit, it signifies appreciation for knowledge and abundance. Celebrate the fruits of your labor and share your blessings with those who value them.

- **Abundance** – Enjoying the fruits of your labor with gratitude.
- **Wisdom** – Recognizing the deeper value of your success.
- **Independence** – Feeling secure and empowered through your achievements.
- **Fulfillment** – Reaching a place of emotional and material satisfaction.
- **Appreciation** – Sharing your blessings with those who value them.

Reversed: Overindulgence or superficiality diminishes the value of your achievements. Neglecting gratitude or humility creates emptiness. This card encourages reflection on the spiritual aspects of success and sharing your wisdom generously.

- **Superficiality** – Overfocusing on material gains undermines deeper fulfillment.
- **Isolation** – Neglecting connection creates emotional emptiness.
- **Greed** – Hoarding success diminishes its value and joy.
- **Discontent** – Feeling unfulfilled despite outward achievements.
- **Neglect** – Overlooking gratitude for blessings disrupts harmony.

Ten of Grains

GOD'S PROMISE TO ABRAHAM

...for all the land that you see,
I will give to you and your offspring forever.
Genesis 13:15 BSB

TEN *of* GRAINS
GOD'S PROMISE TO ABRAHAM (GENESIS 15)

Abram (later known as Abraham) and Lot, journeying together, find that the land cannot support both their flocks and herdsmen, leading to strife. Abram proposes that they separate to avoid conflict, offering Lot the first choice of the land. Lot chooses the fertile plains of Jordan, while Abram dwells in the land of Canaan. God then promises Abram that his descendants will be as numerous as the stars in the sky and that all the land he sees will be given to him and his offspring forever, establishing the foundation for a lasting legacy.

UPRIGHT KEYWORDS:	REVERSED KEYWORDS:
Legacy	Disharmony
Completion	Neglect
Harmony	Stagnation
Gratitude	Fear
Fulfillment	Misalignment

Upright: This card signifies lasting abundance, fulfillment, and divine legacy. Like God's promise to Abraham, it represents blessings that extend beyond yourself to future generations. Embrace the joy of spiritual and material prosperity with gratitude and faith.

- **Legacy** – Building a foundation for future generations to thrive.
- **Completion** – Celebrating the fulfillment of long-term goals and promises.
- **Harmony** – Aligning your material and spiritual life creates peace.
- **Gratitude** – Honoring the blessings and abundance bestowed upon you.
- **Fulfillment** – Experiencing the joy of a divinely guided life.

Reversed: Fear of loss or disconnection from purpose disrupts harmony. Neglecting spiritual values diminishes long-term fulfillment. This card urges you to trust in divine provision and refocus on what truly matters.

- **Disharmony** – Conflicts disrupt the flow of peace and prosperity.
- **Neglect** – Failing to honor commitments weakens your foundation.
- **Stagnation** – Resistance to change blocks progress and legacy-building.
- **Fear** – Doubts about the future diminish present joy.
- **Misalignment** – Prioritizing material gain over spiritual values creates imbalance.

Page of Grains

PRISCILLA - TEACHING THE TEACHERS

And he began to speak boldly in the synagogue.
When Priscilla and Aquila heard him, they took him aside
and explained to him the way of God more accurately.
Acts 18:26 BSB

PAGE *of* GRAINS
PRISCILLA - TEACHING THE TEACHERS (ACTS 18:18-28)

Priscilla and her husband Aquila, tentmakers by trade, meet Paul in Corinth. They work and minister alongside Paul, becoming his close friends and fellow tentmakers. When Paul leaves Corinth, Priscilla and Aquila accompany him to Ephesus. There, they encounter Apollos, who was a persuasive speaker and well-versed in the Scriptures, yet he did not have full understanding of certain matters. Priscilla and Aquila privately guided Apollos, providing him with a more precise understanding of God's teachings. Through their mentorship, Apollos becomes a powerful advocate for Christianity.

UPRIGHT KEYWORDS:	REVERSED KEYWORDS:
Curiosity	Insecurity
Mentorship	Resistance
Creativity	Isolation
Potential	Neglect
Teaching	Frustration

Chapter 26

Upright: This card represents learning, growth, and sharing wisdom. Like Priscilla, it encourages you to embrace opportunities for education and mentorship. Use your knowledge to inspire and guide others on their journey.

- **Curiosity** – Embrace new opportunities to learn and grow.
- **Mentorship** – Share your knowledge to uplift and inspire others.
- **Creativity** – Explore innovative ways to approach challenges.
- **Potential** – Recognize the seeds of growth within yourself and others.
- **Teaching** – Use your insights to guide and nurture those around you.

Reversed: Insecurity or resistance to learning blocks your growth. Fear of sharing your gifts or undervaluing your insights limits potential. This card urges you to trust in your abilities and step confidently into roles of teaching and mentorship.

- **Insecurity** – Doubts about your abilities block growth.
- **Resistance** – Refusing to learn or adapt creates stagnation.
- **Isolation** – Holding back your gifts limits connection and fulfillment.
- **Neglect** – Ignoring your potential hinders progress and purpose.
- **Frustration** – Feeling unrecognized or undervalued stifles creativity.

Knight of Grains

JACOB WORKS FOR LABAN

So Jacob served seven years for Rachel,
yet it seemed but a few days because of his love for her.
Genesis 29:20 BSB

Jacob flees to his uncle Laban's house after deceiving his brother Esau. Upon arriving, Jacob falls in love with Laban's younger daughter, Rachel, and agrees to work for Laban for seven years to marry her. However, Laban deceives Jacob by giving him his older daughter Leah instead, requiring Jacob to serve another seven years for Rachel. Jacob's commitment and hard work over these years, and even beyond, for the wealth he eventually acquires, reflect his determination and resilience.

UPRIGHT KEYWORDS:	REVERSED KEYWORDS:
Perseverance	Burnout
Patience	Frustration
Determination	Impatience
Loyalty	Disconnection
Growth	Resistance

Upright: This card reflects perseverance, dedication, and long-term effort. Like Jacob working for Laban, it symbolizes commitment to achieving your goals through patience and hard work. Trust that persistence will bring rewards.

- **Perseverance** – Committing to hard work leads to long-term rewards.
- **Patience** – Trusting in divine timing despite challenges.
- **Determination** – Staying focused on your goals ensures success.
- **Loyalty** – Honoring commitments builds trust and stability.
- **Growth** – Progress comes from sustained effort and dedication.

Reversed: Frustration or burnout from overwork creates imbalance. Feeling trapped in unfulfilling obligations hinders growth. This card encourages you to reassess your efforts and align them with your values and purpose.

- **Burnout** – Overworking yourself leads to exhaustion and imbalance.
- **Frustration** – Feeling trapped in unfulfilling tasks delays progress.
- **Impatience** – Rushing through work undermines quality and growth.
- **Disconnection** – Losing sight of your purpose creates stagnation.
- **Resistance** – Avoiding commitment blocks meaningful advancement.

Queen of Grains

PROVERBS 31 WOMAN

She perceives that her merchandise is profitable.
Her lamp doesn't go out by night.
Proverbs 31:18 WEB

QUEEN *of* GRAINS
PROVERBS 31 WOMAN (PROVERBS 31:10-31)

Proverbs 31 describes an ideal woman who is virtuous and capable, known for her strong character, wisdom, and industrious nature. She is a diligent homemaker, a savvy businesswoman, and a provider for her family, making her a pillar of strength and stability. Her actions are driven by love and care, and she is respected by her family and community. This passage highlights the value of a woman who fears the Lord and showcases her roles in both the domestic and economic spheres with excellence.

UPRIGHT KEYWORDS:	REVERSED KEYWORDS:
Nurturing	Overextension
Resourcefulness	Resentment
Compassion	Burnout
Strength	Neglect
Faith	Isolation

Upright: This card embodies nurturing, resourcefulness, and wisdom. Like the Proverbs 31 woman, it reflects the ability to create abundance through faith, diligence, and care. Use your gifts to support others while honoring your own needs.

- **Nurturing** – Supporting others with love and wisdom strengthens bonds.
- **Resourcefulness** – Managing resources effectively fosters abundance.
- **Compassion** – Leading with empathy creates harmony and trust.
- **Strength** – Balancing care for others with self-reliance ensures stability.
- **Faith** – Rooting your actions in spiritual values promotes fulfillment.

Reversed: Overextending yourself to meet others' needs leads to exhaustion. Neglecting self-care creates imbalance. This card urges you to set healthy boundaries and nurture yourself alongside others.

- **Overextension** – Neglecting self-care leads to exhaustion and imbalance.
- **Resentment** – Feeling unappreciated diminishes emotional well-being.
- **Burnout** – Overprioritizing others at your expense disrupts harmony.
- **Neglect** – Failing to set boundaries weakens relationships and stability.
- **Isolation** – Withdrawing from support hinders healing and connection.

King of Grains

JOSEPH IN CHARGE OF EGYPT

Pharaoh also told Joseph,
"I hereby place you over all the land of Egypt."
Genesis 41:41 BSB

KING *of* GRAINS
JOSEPH IN CHARGE OF EGYPT (GENESIS 41:41-57)

Joseph, sold into slavery by his brothers, rises to prominence in Egypt through his ability to interpret Pharaoh's dreams, which foretell seven years of abundance followed by seven years of famine. Recognizing Joseph's wisdom, Pharaoh puts him in charge of Egypt's land, tasking him with storing grain during the abundant years to prepare for the famine. Joseph's strategic planning and management save not only Egypt but also the surrounding nations from starvation, ultimately leading to a reunion and reconciliation with his family.

UPRIGHT KEYWORDS:	REVERSED KEYWORDS:
Leadership	Arrogance
Vision	Neglect
Responsibility	Short-Sightedness
Integrity	Imbalance
Abundance	Conflict

Upright: This card represents leadership, vision, and responsibility. Like Joseph's stewardship in Egypt, it reflects the ability to manage resources wisely and inspire others. Lead with integrity and faith to create lasting abundance and stability.

- **Leadership** – Guiding others with wisdom and compassion builds trust.
- **Vision** – Planning for long-term success ensures stability.
- **Responsibility** – Managing resources with care benefits all.
- **Integrity** – Aligning actions with spiritual values promotes peace.
- **Abundance** – Using your gifts to uplift others fosters prosperity.

Reversed: Misuse of power or neglect of responsibilities disrupts harmony. Arrogance or disconnection from purpose weakens leadership. This card encourages reflection on how to align your actions with divine wisdom and care.

- **Arrogance** – Misusing power disrupts harmony and trust.
- **Neglect** – Ignoring responsibilities weakens your leadership.
- **Short-Sightedness** – Prioritizing immediate gains over lasting impact creates instability.
- **Imbalance** – Overfocus on material success disconnects you from purpose.
- **Conflict** – Poor decisions lead to discord and frustration.

Epilogue

Embracing the Shadows, Walking in the Light

The journey of shadow work is a sacred one. It is a path that leads us through the deepest, most hidden parts of our souls, asking us to face the parts of ourselves that we've long denied or buried. Through this process, we come to understand that our shadows are not to be feared, but rather to be embraced as integral parts of who we are.

The Biblical Tarot: Shadows of the Soul has served as a guide through this journey, offering us biblical wisdom and spiritual insight as we wrestle with our inner conflicts and transform our hidden wounds into sources of growth. Each card represents a story, a lesson, a mirror reflecting the complexity of the human spirit. As we've walked alongside figures like Jacob, Moses, David, and others, we've seen how their struggles mirror our own and how their stories offer a blueprint for personal transformation.

Yet, shadow work does not end with the last page of this book or the final tarot reading. It is an ongoing journey—a cyclical process of discovery, reflection, and integration. Life will continue to present us with new challenges, new shadows, and new opportunities to grow. But with the tools you've gained, you are now equipped to navigate these moments with grace, wisdom, and courage.

Living with Compassion for Yourself and Others

As you continue this journey, remember to extend grace and compassion to yourself. Shadow work is not about perfection, nor is it about erasing the parts of yourself that feel difficult or uncomfortable. It is about integration—about becoming whole by accepting both your light and your darkness. In the same way that God extends unconditional love and grace to us, we are called to do the same for ourselves.

As you embrace your shadows, you may also find that your capacity to show compassion to others deepens. The more we understand our own inner struggles, the more empathy we can offer to those around us. By recognizing the shadows within ourselves, we become more aware of the shadows in others, and this awareness can cultivate patience, forgiveness, and love.

Trusting the Process of Transformation

Transformation is not always linear, and it's rarely easy. There will be moments when shadow work feels overwhelming, when the weight of your emotions or the complexity of your inner world seems too much to bear. In those moments, remember the stories of those who came before you—the biblical figures who faced their own darkness and emerged stronger, wiser, and more connected to God.

Jacob's wrestling with God teaches us that struggle is often the gateway to transformation. Just as he emerged from his night of struggle with a new name and a renewed sense of purpose, you too will emerge from your shadow work with a deeper understanding of yourself and your place in the world.

Trust the process. Trust that every shadow you face holds the potential for growth, healing, and redemption. Trust that even in moments of darkness, the light of understanding will eventually break through.

Walking in the Light

As you close this book, you may feel a mixture of emotions—gratitude for the insights you've gained, relief from the burdens you've released, and perhaps even excitement for the continued journey ahead. These feelings are all part of the process of walking in the light.

Shadow work doesn't mean we dwell forever in the darkness. Instead, it teaches us how to carry the light with us, even as we navigate life's inevitable challenges. The lessons you've learned here will serve as your lantern, guiding you through both the shadows and the sunlit paths of life.

Walking in the light means living with greater awareness, compassion, and purpose. It means embracing all parts of yourself, recognizing that your shadows are not separate from who you are but are integral to your growth. It means living in alignment with your highest values and stepping forward with courage, knowing that you are guided by the wisdom of your inner world and the grace of God.

A Blessing for the Journey Ahead

As you continue your journey, may you always be blessed with the courage to face your shadows and the wisdom to learn from them. May you be guided by the light of God's love, even in the darkest moments. And may you walk forward with a heart full of compassion, for yourself and for others, knowing that every step you take brings you closer to wholeness and peace.

This is not the end of the journey; it is only the beginning. Your shadows will continue to teach you, challenge you, and shape you. But now, you walk with the confidence that you have the tools, the guidance, and the grace to navigate this path with strength and clarity.

'

www.ingramcontent.com/pod-product-compliance
Lightning Source LLC
LaVergne TN
LVHW051450080426
835509LV00017B/1719